ENCOUNTERS ON THE PASSAGE:
INUIT MEET THE EXPLORERS

'First communication with the natives of Prince Regents Bay, as drawn by John Sackheouse and Presented to Capt. Ross. Augt 10. 1818.'

ENCOUNTERS
ON THE PASSAGE

Inuit Meet the Explorers

DOROTHY HARLEY EBER

UNIVERSITY OF TORONTO PRESS
Toronto Buffalo London

University of Toronto Press Incorporated
Toronto Buffalo London
www.utppublishing.com
Printed in Canada

ISBN 978-0-8020-9275-5

Printed on acid-free paper

Library and Archives Canada Cataloguing in Publication

Eber, Dorothy
    Encounters on the passage : Inuit meet the explorers / Dorothy Harley Eber.

Includes bibliographical references and index.
ISBN 978-0-8020-9275-5

1. Northwest Passage – Discovery and exploration – British.   2. Inuit –
Nunavut – History.   3. Oral tradition – Nunavut.   4. Explorers – Northwest
Passage – History.   5. Explorers – Nunavut – History.   6. Oral history.   I. Title.

E99.E7E335 2008   910.9163'27   C2008-905150-5

In different form, short sections of this book have appeared in 'Recording the Spirit
World,' *Natural History Magazine* (August 2002); 'Eva Talooki: Her Tribute to Seed
Beads, Long-Time Jewels of the Arctic,' *Innuit Art Quarterly* (Spring 2004); 'A
Chance Encounter with Simon Tookoome,' *Inuit Art Quarterly* (Spring 2001); and
'Rumours of Franklin,' *The Beaver* (June/July 1996).

University of Toronto Press acknowledges the financial assistance to its publishing
program of the Canada Council for the Arts and the Ontario
Arts Council.

University of Toronto Press acknowledges the financial support for its publishing
activities of the Government of Canada through the Book Publishing Industry
Development Program (BPIDP).

Illustration on previous pages: 'First communication with the natives of Prince
Regents Bay, as drawn by John Sackheouse and Presented to Capt. Ross. Augt. 10.
1818.' Sackheouse, a Greenlandic Eskimo who served Ross as an interpreter,
shows Captains John Ross and Edward Parry with the 'wild people,' or Arctic
Highlanders as Ross named them, in Northern Greenland, at the outset of the
British nineteenth-century search for the Northwest Passage.

To the memory of GFE, who gave me the tape recorder, and to the interpreters of the North, past and present, without whose work the written history of the North would be merely a white man's story.

Contents

Acknowledgments

This book draws in the main on personal interviews conducted and tape-recorded in locations across Nunavut, and occasionally on the telephone, from 1994 to 2008. I owe my sincerest thanks to all those I interviewed for so patiently answering my questions. I was fortunate enough to work with amazingly talented interpreters, and I would like to express my admiration for their remarkable skills and my thanks for their major contribution to this book. I am most grateful, too, to have had the opportunity to read and to quote from the transcripts of interviews done with the elders of Igloolik and held in the archives of the Inullariit Elders' Society at the Igloolik Research Centre. Among the able interpreters who assisted me in Nunavut, I particularly want to mention Tommy Anguttitauruq, Lisa Ell Ipeelie, Oleepa Ikidluak, Leah Otak, Louise Anaija, James Pamioyok, and Christopher Amautinuar. I thank also Pia Pootoogook, who sadly died before this book was published, and Papak Panegyuk, both of whom helped with the review of certain sections of tape back in Montreal.

This book depends also on the records, excerpts from which are freely quoted, of expeditions to the Canadian Arctic, from those of Martin Frobisher in the sixteenth century to those of Sir William Edward Parry, Sir John Ross, and Sir Richard Collinson in the nineteenth century, and Roald Amundsen, Vilhjalmur Stefansson, and Knud Rasmussen in the twentieth. I am indebted, too, to the many insights in books on nineteenth-century and early twentieth-century Arctic exploration. Among earlier studies, I would like to mention R.J. Cyriax's *Sir John Franklin's Last Arctic Expedition* (London: Methuen & Co. 1939), still one of the best books on the Franklin tragedy, and L.P. Kirwan's *The White Road* (London: Hollis & Carter, 1959). Particularly helpful among more recent publications have been Ann Savours's *The Search for the North West Passage* (New York: St Martin's Press, Scholarly and Reference Division, 1999); Fergus Fleming's *Barrow's Boys* (New York: Atlantic Monthly Press, 1998); Robert Ruby's *Unknown Shore: The Lost History of England's Arctic Colony* (New York: Henry Holt and Company, 2001); M.J. Ross's *Polar Pioneers* (Montreal and Kingston: McGill-Queen's University Press, 1994); and Roland Huntford's *Scott and Amundsen* (London: Hodder and Stoughton, 1979). I must also acknowledge a debt to David C. Woodman's *Unravelling the Franklin Mystery* (Montreal and Kingston: McGill-Queen's University Press, 1991). This study of the Inuit testimony given to the nineteenth-century searchers who looked for the lost Franklin expedition made me wonder whether present-day Inuit might still have stories to tell.

I am grateful to the airline Canadian North for its very practical assistance in helping me reach remote locations in Canada's Arctic. I also owe thanks to the McLennan Library of McGill University, where I consulted the volumes in the Rare Book Room and on the shelves of G 585 to G 875 for several years. I would particularly like to thank John Mac-Donald, director of the Igloolik Research Centre during my visit, for ongoing assistance, Tessa Macintosh of Yellowknife for help in locating photographic material, Susan Rowley for generously giving me access to one of her own interviews, Ann Savours Shirley for help with a troublesome footnote, Dr Paul Pross and Kenn Harper for assistance in locating material, Dr Edmund Carpenter for lending me early Inuit illustrative work, Dr Rui de Sousa for a helpful discussion on Hellenic oral history, and Tom Irvine, formerly of the Royal Canadian Navy, for information on recent transits of the Northwest Passage. Thanks also to my agent Beverley Slopen, to all at University of Toronto Press, and to Elizabeth Gibson, who lent sharp eyes to a check of the page proofs.

Finally, I want to express my gratitude to those who read the manuscript and offered important suggestions, particularly Merloyd Lawrence, Lesley Andrassy, John MacDonald, and Dr Russell Potter.

Dorothy Harley Eber
Montreal, 2008

Introduction

'They were walking inland, walking the mainland – the *nunamariq* – "the real land." They were a raggedy bunch and their clothing was not well made. Their skins were black and the meat above their teeth was gone; their eyes were gaunt. Were they *tuurngait* – spirits – or what?'

From a high-rise office in Iqaluit, Cathy Towtongie, a member of one of the old Inuit whaling families and today a busy Nunavut executive, is recounting the story she heard as a child from her grandmother, of Sir John Franklin's men in their hour of desperation. 'It was a bedtime story,' she says, a little incredulously. 'When I got scared, I pulled on the braids.'

The story came from her grandmother Kanyuk Bruce of Coral Harbour, and Cathy Towtongie's own great-grandfather, Meliki – 'the American' – so called because he worked for the Americans, is among those who probably disseminated this startlingly clinical description. A famous whaler and dog-team traveller, Meliki went on one of the overland Franklin searches that Americans undertook during the second half of the nineteenth century and met Inuit who encountered these dying men.[1]

Across Nunavut, after more than 150 years, these spectral marchers still have power to raise shivers. 'They starved,' the Igloolik elder Rosie Iqallijuq told me. 'They starved even though they were white men.'

I first heard Inuit tell their stories of explorers who came to their lands in the nineteenth and the early twentieth centuries to seek a Northwest Passage in the vast jigsaw jumble of the Arctic archipelago one summer in the mid-1990s. Other work had brought me to the Arctic Ocean coast[2] and on a bright July day, I flew over the easy-access Arctic of today – from Coppermine to Cambridge Bay to Gjoa Haven to Taloyoak (which used to be called Spence Bay). In the regions beneath us, Franklin's men had died. Yet, in sight from the Twin Otter, gleaming below us, were miles and miles of ice-free ocean. How tantalizingly attainable, I thought, the Northwest Passage, the goal of centuries, must at times have seemed.

It was the memory of that ice-free water, brilliant in twenty-four-hour daylight, that caused me to put one more question to Lena King-miatook at the end of our interview next day. From her perspective as an elder, Lena had been talking about the laws of Canada, and their value for communities like Taloyoak now that Inuit live 'the new way.' For the first time, I was working with Tommy Anguttitauruq, a highly trained legal interpreter, and I had already turned off the tape recorder when the thought occurred: 'Tell me,' I asked, 'did you ever hear stories of Franklin?'

Sir John Franklin and a full complement of officers and men aboard the vessels *Erebus* and *Terror* sailed from England in 1845 on the last expedition the British Royal Navy sent specifically in quest of a water-way to the East across North America, and were last sighted by Euro-pean eyes in Baffin Bay. The many expeditions that went in search of them (and eventually mapped several passages) found ample evidence of disaster, but the story of what actually happened to Franklin's men and his ships remains unclear. Investigators and armchair historians regularly return to the puzzle.

Inuit who met the early searchers – John Rae in 1854, Sir Leopold McClintock in 1859, the Americans Charles Francis Hall in 1864–9 and Lieutenant Frederick Schwatka in 1879, and even Greenlander Knud Rasmussen in 1923 – had stories to tell. But could present-day Inuit have any knowledge of such long-ago events? When Lena and I do our interviews together, the new Canadian territory of Nunavut is not far in the future. The pace of change is rapid. Television is on in every house. Inuit children study the computer. As is the case for children all over the world, their culture is increasingly cyber culture.

But my long-shot question was a lucky one. After a rapid-fire Inukti-tut exchange, Tommy explains: 'That was long before Lena was born, but Lena has heard the stories passed down from one person to another from her late husband, who was raised by old people. Her stories are of ships that couldn't get to where they wanted to go and couldn't go back.' Then Lena demonstrates the strength of the Inuit oral tradition up to today. She begins to tell the story of how one group of Inuit – the Netsilik, who had never before met white people – prepared them-selves to meet strange beings unlike any ever seen before, after they

The Gjoa Haven artist Judas Ullulaq with a carving he told photographer Tessa Macintosh represents 'the shaman who first saw a ship.' The shaman was Qiqtutunuaruq, who identified the creatures on John Ross's *Victory* as 'qallunaat' – white people. He returned from his trance with a tea leaf on his tongue.

were sighted by one of their number at the place Inuit still call today Kablunaaqhiuvik – 'the place for meeting white people.'

'That night everyone was quite scared, not knowing what was in their hunting territory. They all gathered in one of the igloos with quite a few of their shamans so they could try to find out. Qiqtutunuaruq was the most powerful shaman, and when he went into his trance, he told the Inuit that what they had seen were qallunaat – white people. He said, "We don't have to be afraid of them." Next morning it was very clear and wonderful weather, and so they decided to walk over. The shaman had told them the qallunaat were not dangerous, not to be scared; they were only white people; they were not dangerous.

'One man said, "We should have war with these people," but the other Inuit said, "If we have war, we're not winning. As long as they're peaceful people, not violent or aggressive, let's be the way they are. We won't lose any men and they won't lose men either." Just in case something didn't go right, they took along their long spears with blades of bone or antler. As they got closer, these big people from the ship came out and the Inuit all lined up. They probably were expecting something worse, so they were ready. The shaman told his people "Maniktumiq – do it smoothly, not aggressively." The Inuit all stood together and said the same word – Maniktumiq – do it smoothly. It was sort of a prayer to a greater power; a prayer to the spirit. All together they began walking gently and smoothly, not aggressively.'

This is indeed a wonderful story, but it does not concern Franklin. Rather, it describes the first encounter of the Netsilik with the expedition of the earlier explorer John Ross. Beset with his vessel the *Victory* through the winters of 1830, '31, and '32 on the east coast of the Boothia Peninsula, Ross met the Inuit in January 1830 and published his own account of the event, illustrated with a coloured engraving made from his own watercolour, a new technique at the time. 'As I approached, the whole party came suddenly out of their shelter, forming in a body of ten in front and three deep … Proceeding then alone, to within a hundred yards, I found that each was armed with a spear and a knife, but saw no bows and arrows.'[3]

In Lena's bungalow, with television on in the background, I was hearing essentially the same story John Ross told in his book, but from the Inuit point of view. For Tommy and me, Lena's story was an epic as dramatic as opera. We kept the tape recorder on and she told us more.

Since hearing Lena's stories, I have attempted my own Northwest Passage, travelling with my tape recorder in hopes of recording more accounts of the explorers' sojourns in their territory which some Inuit – perhaps not for much longer – still can tell. Why did I find these stories so fascinating? Perhaps simply because they tell another side of the story. In the South, the conquest of the Arctic regions is justly recounted as a saga of heroic proportions. But what was it like for Inuit who had to summon deep depths of daring to meet the explorers, generally the first white men encountered, and suspected those terrifying pale faces were spirits – or ghosts? Inuit oral history gives us some answers – and a picture of the Inuit world at the moment before it changed forever. Inuit often talk about the explorers' gifts of beads and tea and metal – but the explorers brought much, much more. They carried with them the virus of new thinking – they were the vectors of irrevocable change.

With its terrible death toll and mysteries still unsolved, for southern audiences the Franklin saga dominates accounts of nineteenth-century Arctic exploration, but in the central Arctic, I quickly found, the canon of Inuit oral history gives centre stage to the specific expeditions of William Edward Parry (1821–3), John Ross (1829–33), and the Norwegian Roald Amundsen (1903–6). These were explorers with whom the Inuit had close contact. But Inuit do retain Franklin stories – important ones. People who study oral history sometimes say that every interview is an exploration. This became more than metaphor for me when I met and interviewed Inuit with information that appears to significantly alter our knowledge of the end of the Franklin expedition. Inuit oral history about 'the ship at Imnguyaaluk' – a place, I learn, 'called after a shaman who died there long before white men came to the North' – and about 'the fireplace trail,' adds a new chapter to the Franklin tragedy.

My first port of call was Iqaluit, now Nunavut's boom town (QUALITY EXECUTIVE CONDOS – buy or rent – Residential and Commercial! RESERVE NOW) on the bay where Martin Frobisher arrived in 1576. He believed that in the bay, which he 'named after his name, Frobisher Streytes, like Magellanus at the Southweast ende of the worlde,'[4] he had found the Passage and also gold. Both were delusions, but his voyages launched a centuries-long era of searches for a Northwest Passage. Around the time I interviewed Lena, a colleague had told me that some Inuit here still retained oral history relating to Frobisher's visits, and indeed they did.[5]

After Frobisher, mariners continued to search for a Northwest Passage. Between 1585 and 1587, John Davis rediscovered Greenland and found the strait named after him. In 1616 the great sailor William Baffin rounded Baffin Bay and glimpsed the waters he called Jones Sound, Smith Sound, and Lancaster Sound. (All so-called sounds would prove to be open waterways.) Early in the seventeenth century, Henry Hudson sailed through Hudson Strait and discovered Hudson Bay, and here, and in connected waters, more searchers – Thomas James, Luke Fox, Jens Munk, and others – pursued the goal. Perhaps Inuit traditions pertaining to their voyages exist, or did until fairly recent times (see Appendix 1), but the stories and information I collect, and which appear here, come from Britain's great century of Arctic exploration, the nineteenth, and the first years of the twentieth, when the search moved to higher latitudes, into the Arctic archipelago.

In various summers, I visit Igloolik, go back to Taloyoak, on to Pelly Bay and Gjoa Haven, and twice to Cambridge Bay (with a side trip to

Inuit in not-so-long-ago camp days. *Beginning a Journey,* stone cut print by Hannah Kigusiuq, Baker Lake, 1972.

Baker Lake, where former Back River people live, now the only inland Inuit community). People in these Arctic Ocean coast communities, until the move to the settlements in the 1950s and 1960s, had their camps all over the regions where the dramas of the British explorers played out, and where, at long last, the Norwegian Roald Amundsen successfully completed the transit of the Northwest Passage by sea. Wherever I go, I find great storytellers – and great artists: since Inuit became town dwellers, their artworks, which depict the lifestyles and beliefs that sustained them for millennia, have astonished the world.

One year, Gjoa Haven on King William Island is my particular focus. Here I have the opportunity to work again with Tommy Anguttitauruq (Gjoa Haven is his hometown). It was on the island's west coast that Leopold (later Sir Leopold) McClintock and his second-in-command, First Lieutenant William Hobson, discovered the only written record ever found of the lost Franklin expedition. On King William Island, Franklin's crews dropped as they walked, sometimes, a woman tells me, bartering silver spoons as they struggled on. Here, just over fifty years later, Roald Amundsen planned for success. He spent two winters here in the harbour he named Gjoa Haven, after his small fishing smack. Today the home-away-from-home for visiting qallunaat is the Amundsen Hotel. A waitress, curious about my work, asks, 'Are you collecting those old fairy stories?' I tell her I do hope to hear old stories. But they are not fairy stories. Much Inuit oral history parallels the explorers' written records, offering correlations and contrasts, and, always, new perspectives.

Many stories I collect suggest how terrifying the white explorers were. Their long pale faces made them 'otherworldly.' Today the Inuit are Christians – Anglicans, Catholics, or sometimes members of new fundamentalist congregations – but before the missionaries brought Christianity, says Mabel Angulalik of Cambridge Bay, 'We looked to the shamans for help.' Shamans, or *angakkuit*, play starring roles in the interaction between Inuit and the explorers – 'the strangers intruding on the Inuit land.' Potential for violence is always there and there are well-documented accounts of attacks against sixteenth- and seventeenth-century explorers.[6] (Blood feuds and revenge murders were common in Inuit societies into the twentieth century.) But in stories of the Parry, Ross, and Amundsen expeditions, Inuit opt for peaceful relations – 'If we have war, we're not winning' – and gain access to the white man's plenty – metal and other culture-altering goods.

In these stories, the cosmogony of the old Inuit world is still in place. Shamans were the regulators of the Inuit world, the mediators between humans and the spirit realm. They were said to fly through the air to faraway places, assume animal forms, cure human sickness, and make animals plentiful when people were hungry. They gained their powers through inheritance or a 'calling' or rigorous initiation. They were assisted by *tuurngait*, their spirit helpers, who were the souls of animals but could also be souls of inanimate objects such as rocks, mountains, or icebergs. A shaman might receive *tuurngait* through inheritance, as a gift from his tutor at the time of initiation, or he might have to suffer greatly to induce a spirit to come to him. Tommy Anguttitauruq, a grandson of the great western Arctic shaman Alikamik, told me a little about how a *tuurngait* attached himself to a shaman. 'They say the spirit chooses. Sometimes in different regions a person becoming a shaman had to go through very, very unpleasant things. Some would suffer for a long time – they might be asking for a spirit to help them for days and days. I believe the mind focuses on the spirit, nothing but the spirit, for days and days; finally the spirit agrees to help. After that it becomes quite easy to ask the spirit for help.'

Tommy Anguttitauruq explained how the old stories were passed on. Even for his generation, the last born and raised at least partially on the land, stories were a major source of entertainment. 'In those days there was lots of time to tell stories, no television, no radio, no restaurants. The stories were very important. We memorized them and so that way we could pass them on.' Like academic history, Inuit history is subject to error and interpretation – and Inuit have revisionists, too. 'Every time the stories are told, maybe they're a little bit different; there's a little bit added and maybe some things not said.'

Inuit treasure these stories. Not long before his death, the King William Island sculptor Judas Ullulaq made a carving which represented, he told Yellowknife photographer Tessa Macintosh, 'the shaman who first saw a ship.' The ship was the *Victory*; the shaman, Qiqtutunuaruq, from Lena's story, who identified the strange creatures aboard as qallunaat – white people. It is said he returned from his trance with a tea leaf on his tongue, a portent of the riches in the white man's gift.

Some of the stories Inuit tell here are new to English-speaking readers; others echo and sometimes expand on stories told to Sir Leopold McClintock, Charles Francis Hall, and William H. Gilder, that investigative reporter who accompanied the Schwatka expedition a thousand miles by dog team to report for his newspaper. In the twentieth century, Knud Rasmussen and the Hudson's Bay Company (HBC) factor L.A. Learmonth also heard the stories.[7] All these accounts represent remarkable reporting; there were no portable lightweight tape recorders then. In contrast, we who do interviews in the North today have increasingly sophisticated recording tools with manifold advantages.

It would be naïve to believe, however, that the Inuit oral tradition can retain its vigour and validity in the face of the new lifestyles and southern influences that flood the North today. Storytellers like Lena Kingmiatook, whom I had the luck to meet in Taloyoak, are rare. When I arrive in a community, I often wish I had been in time to talk to storytellers of the frustratingly recent past. In Cambridge Bay, I was told that the story of the ship at Imnguyaaluk had originally been Patsy Topilikton's story and that he had been able to tell it in a fuller manner with greater detail. But Patsy Topilikton died some years before my arrival. Some stories I hear in a number of forms. For instance, the story of Abiluktuq, the first of the Netsilik to see John Ross's *Victory*, who ran home as fast as his legs could carry him, is told today with much laughter all over the region, sometimes, perhaps because of its popularity, in connection with other expeditions (although Ross makes its provenance clear as can the elders of Pelly Bay whose ancestors visited the ship). Old stories are sometimes blended together or 'collapsed,' as anthropologists say, a process apparently much on the increase in the last fifteen years. John MacDonald, at the time of my visit director of the Igloolik Research Centre, says that until rather recent times, over wide areas and through long stretches of time, classic stories were repeated with amazing consistency. He asks, 'Is the ability to retain changing now that people write things down? Stories considered legends were once required to be learned almost by rote. These stories are now getting through to the next generation only in a fragmented state. "A neat story" is how young people describe epic stories incorporating Inuit cosmology. But elders are not pleased, because the stories "are all mixed up." They say, "They should not change; they should be told just the same."'

To echo John MacDonald's question: Is the ability to retain changing now that people write things down? This was Plato's question when through the fifth and fourth centuries BC literacy spread and became general, making the storytellers' great feats of hour after hour of recitation unnecessary. The ancients saved their stories – through reading and writing. In the modern North, the oral tradition will need the new technologies of our time to survive.

Fortunately, since 1986, members of the Inullariit Elders' Society in Igloolik in wide-ranging interviews, conducted and transcribed for the most part by younger bilingual Inuit, have recorded stories, songs, customs, and traditions for a pioneering oral history program. Since the first interviews were recorded, many of the contributors have died, but their stories are alive in the Society's archives in the Igloolik Research Centre. More recently, other communities also have begun oral history projects – Gjoa Haven and Baker Lake among them. For the moment, in communities across Nunavut, older Inuit still have information and are generous with it, believing it important to preserve an Inuit record.

Their collaboration gives new dimensions – an Inuit point of view and Inuit voice – to the story of the search for the Northwest Passage.

On exhibit in Gjoa Haven is a bronze bust of Roald Amundsen. Nearby you find a weathered log, a presumed relic of a Franklin vessel. I see them the day I arrive in Gjoa Haven, and soon after I go with Tommy to visit his mother, Alice Anguttitauruq. Like many elders in this community, she can make history come alive. In her childhood, she says, her parents used to talk about the doomed strangers in strange clothing – 'all black, no fur' – who had appeared on the shore of King William Island about seventy-five years before her birth. 'Not many Inuit saw them, but people passed on the stories they heard from others. In those times on the southwest side of King William Island there were always Inuit out hunting seal. Sometimes they saw strange creatures, strange beings wearing dark clothing, pulling a small object behind them. When the Inuit saw them, they thought they were spirits. They would never go close – they were always afraid. They thought they were spirits because the people of that time had never really heard of the white man.'

For the moment, Inuit oral history still rivets attention.

Chronology and Maps of Principal Nineteenth- and Early Twentieth-Century Arctic Expeditions by Sea

1818 John Ross sails round Baffin Bay on the British Admiralty's first nineteenth-century expedition to seek a Northwest Passage above continental North America but fails to discover the entrance to Lancaster Sound.

1819–20 William Edward Parry sails victoriously through Lancaster Sound and winters far to the west at Melville Island. No one will sail farther west for thirty years.

1821–3 Parry seeks a Northwest Passage closer to the North American mainland and overwinters twice, spending the second winter at Igloolik. He cannot penetrate the ice of Fury and Hecla Strait but has close contact with the Inuit.

1824 Parry's former second-in-command, George F. Lyon, makes an unsuccessful voyage to Repulse Bay, narrowly avoiding losing his ship.

1824–5 Parry makes his final attempt to find a Northwest Passage through the Arctic archipelago, leaving the *Fury* along with her stores at Fury Beach in Prince Regent Inlet, thus saving the lives of John Ross and his men seven years later.

1829–33 John Ross takes a privately financed expedition on his steam vessel *Victory* down Prince Regent Inlet to Kablunaaqhiuvik – 'the place for meeting white people' – in the Thom Bay area. He abandons his ship after three winters in the ice. He and his men trek to Fury Beach, where they spend a fourth winter, then row into Lancaster Sound and are rescued by whalers.

1836–7 George Back makes an unsuccessful voyage into Wager Bay and sails home in a ruined ship.

1845–7   Sir John Franklin goes in search of the Northwest Passage with the *Erebus* and the *Terror*. After encounters with whalers in Baffin Bay, they are never seen again by Western eyes.

1848–54   Massive search expeditions, British and American, naval and private, search by sea from the east and from the west for the lost Franklin expedition. These expeditions are considered to have numbered in the vicinity of forty by the time they end.

1853   Robert McClure, searching from the west, abandons his vessel *Investigator* on the coast of Banks Island and with his crew completes a transit of the Northwest Passage on foot.

1850–5   Richard Collinson makes the longest of all search expeditions, sailing from the Pacific past Russian Alaska and wintering twice on Victoria Island, the second time at Cambridge Bay. Inuit seem to bring him news, but he has no interpreter and cannot understand them. He comes within miles of finding evidence of the lost Franklin expedition.

1857–9   Jane, Lady Franklin, with friends, finances the expedition of Leopold McClintock and the voyage of the *Fox*. The expedition finds a note in a cairn on the northwest coast of King William Island, which establishes Sir John Franklin's death on 11 June 1847 and abandonment of the *Erebus* and the *Terror* on 22 April 1848.

1903–6   The Norwegian Roald Amundsen with his fishing smack the *Gjoa* makes the first Northwest Passage by sea.

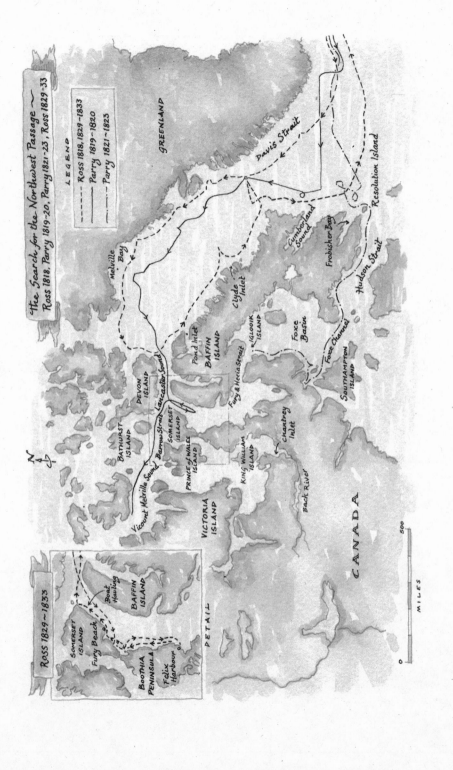

The Search for the Northwest Passage —
Ross 1818, Parry 1819-20, Parry 1821-23, Ross 1829-33

LEGEND

- - - - Ross 1818, 1829-1833
———— Parry 1819-1820
– – – Parry 1821-1825

GREENLAND

Davis Strait

Resolution Island

Cumberland Sound

Frobisher Bay

Hudson Strait

Melville Bay

Clyde Inlet

Pond Inlet

BAFFIN ISLAND

Igloolik ISLAND

Foxe Basin

Southampton ISLAND

Foxe Channel

DEVON ISLAND

Lancaster Sound

Fury & Hecla Strait

Chantrey Inlet

Back River

BATHURST ISLAND

Barrow Strait

SOMERSET ISLAND

PRINCE of WALES ISLAND

KING WILLIAM ISLAND

Viscount Melville Sound

VICTORIA ISLAND

CANADA

N

ROSS 1829-1833

SOMERSET ISLAND

Fury Beach

Boat Hauling

BAFFIN ISLAND

BOOTHIA PENINSULA

Felix Harbour

DETAIL

MILES

0   500

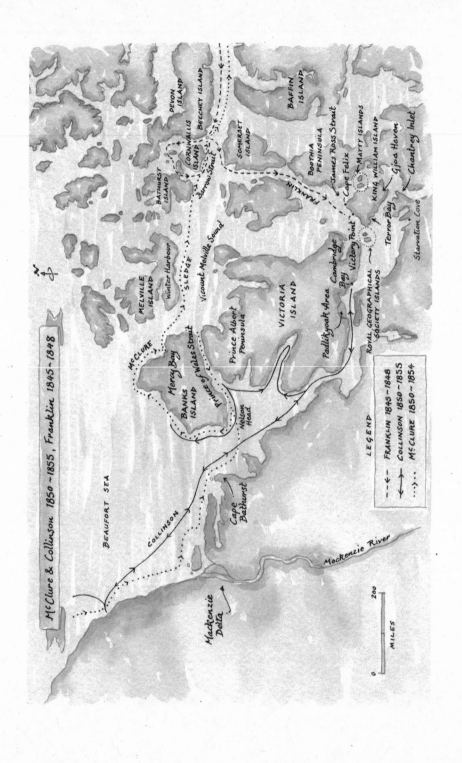

McClure & Collinson 1850~1855, Franklin 1845~1848

N

BEAUFORT SEA

Mackenzie Delta

Mackenzie River

Cape Bathurst

COLLINSON

Nelson Head

BANKS ISLAND

Mercy Bay

McCLURE

Prince of Wales Strait

Prince Albert Peninsula

MELVILLE ISLAND

Winter Harbour

SLEDGE

Viscount Melville Sound

BATHURST ISLAND

CORNWALLIS ISLAND

Barrow Strait

DEVON ISLAND

BEECHEY ISLAND

SOMERSET ISLAND

BAFFIN ISLAND

BOOTHIA PENINSULA

James Ross Strait

Cape Felix

MATTY ISLANDS

KING WILLIAM ISLAND

Gjoa Haven

Chantrey Inlet

Terror Bay

Starvation Cove

Victory Point

ROYAL GEOGRAPHICAL SOCIETY ISLANDS

FRANKLIN

VICTORIA ISLAND

Padliak Area

Cambridge Bay

LEGEND

--←-- Franklin 1845~1848
——→ Collinson 1850~1855
·····›· McClure 1850~1854

0   200

MILES

ENCOUNTERS ON THE PASSAGE:
INUIT MEET THE EXPLORERS

Map of the north polar regions, by Christopher Weigel (1654–1725).

Prologue: Opening Salvos

On the 7th of June, a Thursday, in 'the year of our Lord 1576,' Martin Frobisher sailed out with the *Gabriel*, the *Michael*, and a pinnace – the pinnace would sink and the *Michael* shortly turn back – on the search for a 'Straight or passage to China.' The expedition headed down the Thames, pausing at Greenwich, where the Queen was in residence, and, says Christopher Hall, master of the *Gabriel*, 'bare down by the Court, where we shot off our ordinance, and made the best show we could. Her Majesty, beholding the same, commended it, and bade us farewell with shaking her hand at us out of the window.'[1]

More than four centuries later, in Iqaluit in the new Canadian territory of Nunavut, I wait, my tape recorder in my hand, for Inookie Adamie to relate what happened after that royal farewell.

And Inookie begins: 'During the first meeting, the Inuit were just in awe. The qallunaat came with their huge ship. The Inuit themselves had only sealskin boats – the kayak made from sealskins and the umiaq – the women's boat, called that way because it was sewn by the women – made from square flippers. They had never seen a ship. They had never heard a shot.

'Right away, there were some conflicts. Because they weren't quite Inuit. When the ship was spotted, the Inuit took their kayaks and went to meet the ship. They had never seen such a big ship and the people were strange, just different. Right away there were some grudges. The qallunaat fired two warning shots in the air. I'm sure the qallunaat had good intentions, but they had never seen Inuit before and Inuit had never seen qallunaat.

'So when they met there was a lot of uncertainty. The Inuit were scared. They didn't want to give in to these people because they didn't know what they were. Because they weren't quite Inuit. And their clothes – how they dressed! The Inuit dressed in sealskin or caribou skins. The qallunaat looked so different. They were different beings. The Inuit had never seen clothes like that. Eventually we decided the first explorers basically were dressed in rags. This was partly because we knew their clothes would never protect them from the cold. But Inuit had never met qallunaat so it was partly later, after seeing later white men, that we thought they were poorly dressed, that they more or less wore rags. At first contact Inuit thought, "How come they dress like this?" It's very cold; their clothes are not fit for this kind of weather. They used to wonder ... They were ghostly.'

For a moment longer, Frobisher's shots down the bay still echo in oral history. Inookie, his uncle Lucassie Nowdlak (four years his senior but somewhat deaf, so he lets Inookie do the talking), and Udluriak Inneak, a lively older woman confined to a wheelchair, are the last in Iqaluit to have heard the old stories – passed on through centuries – in camps on the shores of Frobisher Bay. Our interpreters are Oleepa Ikidluak, a legal interpreter, and, helping out because of her interest, CBC producer Lisa Ell Ipeelie.[2] As a little girl, she went along when in 1974 her father, Ben Ell, took the first archaeologist, Walter Kenyon of the Royal Ontario Museum, by boat to sites on the bay where Frobisher's men explored and 'looked for nuggets.'

In Frobisher's day, the merchants of England had need of a North-west Passage, a waterway to the Orient across Arctic America. Other routes to the East and its wealth were controlled by the Spanish and the Portuguese, with their rights sanctioned by the Pope. Frobisher sailed financed by willing venture capitalists, and when he entered Frobisher Bay, he believed he was well on the way to success. He judged he had America on the south side and Asia on the north.

Christopher Hall, chief pilot for all of Frobisher's voyages, gives a first-hand account of the first meeting with the Inuit: 'The 19th day in the morning being calm and no wind, ... the captain and I took our boat, with eight men in her, to row us ashore, to see if there were any people, or no, and going to the top of the island, we had sight of seven boats, which came rowing from the east side ...' Of the people, Hall says, 'They be like Tartars, with long black hair, broad faces, and flat noses, and tawny in colour, wearing sealskins; and so do the women; not differing in fashion; but the women are marked in the face with blue streaks down the cheeks, and round about the eyes.'

At first all seemed to go well between the Inuit and the strangers. Might they be ghosts? The Inuit visited the ship and did acrobatics in the ropes, but when Frobisher sent five seamen to deliver an Inuk visitor ashore, the Inuit captured the men and took the ship's boat. 'The next day, in the morning,' writes Hall, 'we stood in near the shore and shot off a *fauconet* and sounded our trumpet; but we could hear nothing of our men.'[3] Without his boat, Frobisher could not reach shore to look for his boat crew, and without them he had hardly enough men to bring his vessel home. He remained four days and then left. He took with him an Inuk he captured by force, proof of the new country he had discovered.[4]

Frobisher sailed home and became 'specially famous for the great hope he brought of the passage to Cataya.'[5] But from this first voyage, along with his captured Inuk, he had also brought a rock which assayers said held gold. The next year, with a larger expedition – the *Gabriel* and the *Michael* and a tall ship, the *Ayde*, lent by the Queen herself – he sailed again to the territory Queen Elizabeth now called Meta Incognita. Backers and support increased, but 'The Captain' was 'more specially directed' to searching for gold than for 'any further discovery of the passage.'[6]

The Second Voyage

Frobisher explored and excavated on the American and supposed Asian sides of the bay and headquartered his expedition on an island known today as Kodlunarn Island – white men's island – about 25 acres in size and down the bay 115 miles from Iqaluit. Here his miners mined a promising vein, while Inuit watched from a vantage point on the nearby mainland.

Perhaps it was then that Inuit first recognized the white man's obsession with the shiny metal. In the middle of the twentieth century, walking past a river where underwater rocks glittered in the sun, Alikamik, the great shaman of the Perry River area, told his grandson, 'Never show that to the qallunaat – it steals their minds.'[7]

Relations between the Inuit and the Elizabethans continued to be bad, characterized by hostage-taking and attempted hostage-taking. (Frobisher still hoped to rescue or ransom his lost men.) They reached their nadir at Bloody Point. When the Englishmen came upon a group of Inuit on land, the Inuit jumped into boats to escape but then met a pinnace with a crew of white men. The Inuit, cornered, went back to land and ran to the top of a cliff. Says Inookie, 'The old stories say that the Inuit were so terrified of these white men in the rowboats that thinking they were not of this world, they started shooting arrows at them.'

The English shot arrows back, wounding three. 'Perceiving themselves thus hurt, they desperately leaped off the rocks into the sea and drowned themselves ... Two women not being so apt to escape as the men were, the one for her age, and the other being incumbered with a young child, we took. The old wretch, whom divers of our sailors supposed to be either a devil or a witch, had her buskins plucked off to see if she were cloven-footed, and for her ugly hue and deformity we let her go. The young woman and child we brought away. We named the place where they were slain Bloody Point ...'[8]

Nearby in Inuit tents, the Englishmen find the clothes of their five lost men, arrows through them. George Best, Frobisher's lieutenant, writes, 'We began to suspect we had heard the last news of our men.'[9]

The Third Voyage

Some assays of the rocks from the second voyage were better than others, but Frobisher sailed again on a third voyage with what is still the largest fleet ever sent to the Canadian Arctic – fifteen vessels carrying some four hundred men. At Kodlunarn Island, ten years before settlement in Virginia, fifty years before the *Mayflower* landed the pilgrims in Massachusetts, Queen Elizabeth ordered Frobisher to set up a colony. It was planned that one hundred men, among them many miners, would winter over on Kodlunarn Island in a prefabricated fort.

Kodlunarn Island has been described as 'flat, rock-strewn and barren.'[10] But Inuit do not see it that way. Wheelchair-bound Udluriak Inneak, who, like her contemporary Inookie Adamie, spent her youth on the shores of the mainland near the island, says, 'If I had a skidoo, I'd go right there now. We made a lot of use of the island when I was growing up because it was a good-for-anchoring area. A lot of times, hunters would go out after seal, anchor their boats, and then go up on the island and start shooting seals from the island. But it was not just for seals, it was a good hunting spot, a good gathering spot. A lot of times there were duck there and we ate the duck eggs, very handy to have. It was also used when the seasons changed – the area in fall was good for hunting walrus, and when travelling by dog team, that spot was a good place to gather. It was an excellent hunting ground, abun-

The battle at Bloody Point in 1577. 'The old stories say that the Inuit were so terrified of these white men in the rowboats, that thinking they were not of this world, they started shooting arrows at them,' says Inookie Adamie of Iqaluit. Drawn by or after John White.

dant in walrus and seal, and a good spot to be in winter, recognized by the hunters as a spot that kept their bellies full. We used the island a lot when I was young because of it being a good anchorage, but also, because the land was so beautiful, we liked to go there a lot.'

As it turned out, Queen Elizabeth's ambitious plans for settlement had to be abandoned. Frobisher's fleet reached Kodlunarn Island late in the summer, since by mistake many vessels – including Frobisher's – had sailed into Hudson Strait, where in foul weather one vessel was lost and others suffered damage. And part of the 'parcel' of the prefabricated building was lost at sea. However, Frobisher's men built and left behind a blacksmith's shop, an assay shop, and a brick house, fourteen by twelve feet with two-foot thick walls, which seems to have had a tiled roof. And still prominent on the island today are mine excavations, which Inuit call the ship's trench and the reservoir; and, not far away by water, is a cliff with no particular identifying features except its name – Naparuqsivik – 'where the poles were put up.'

Udluriak Inneak recalls the stories elders told: 'They used to talk about the Queen's people. How they used Kodlunarn Island for their boat – their big boat. They had this deep trench and used it to repair their boat. And also they had a water supply area. And the building they made for themselves. And also there was a place on a cliffside where they fixed their masts. That's how it got its name "Naparuqsivik" – where the poles are set up. That name is still in use today.'

Inookie Adamie says, 'The house was demolished long ago; there are only foundations now, but there were always people living around so for sure my ancestors saw it. My grandfather told stories about how they repaired a ship over there in the trench. They made the hollow so the ship could be pulled up there for repairs. Then after they'd finished repairing, they towed the ship to another place to fix the masts. They towed the big ship by boat to Naparuqsivik. There are a lot of stories about that place. The small islands across from Naparuqsivik are called Naujaaruluk – "small seagulls." At the cliff, they put the masts into the ship. There were people with ropes on the top of the cliff and they lowered the masts into the ship. They were quite heavy. I've heard the story many times. I know it's true.'

Frobisher's lieutenant, George Best, wrote that he arrived at Kodlunarn Island with his vessel the *Anne Francis* on 28 August, and on 30 August she 'was brought aground and had eight great leaks mended.'[11]

Best does not specify that the repair took place in the mined trench, but archaeologists have found wood chips consistent with boat repair or construction.[12]

As the fleet got ready to depart, masons finished the house, and, says George Best, who had been under fire from Inuit arrows just days before, 'the better to allure those brutish and uncivil people to courtesy against other times of our coming, we left therein divers of our country toys, as bells and knives, wherein they specially delight, one for necessary use, and the other for the great pleasure thereof ...'[13]

On the 1578 homeward journey, Frobisher's fleet carried great cargoes of rock from Kodlunarn Island and other sites around the bay. But the more than thousand tons so arduously extracted did not contain gold. The rock was fool's gold and on arrival was unceremoniously dumped overboard or used for building. Frobisher returned to disaster: lawsuits, rumours of chicanery, bankruptcy for some of the backers, and financial losses for all. The Queen was among the losers, but Frobisher retained her favour. He fought with Drake in the defeat of the Spanish Armada and was knighted on deck after battle.

After Frobisher's third voyage, no more expeditions sailed for Kodlunarn Island. There was certainly no interest in Frobisher's mines – the lawsuits continued for years – and the exact position of 'Frobisher's Straight' was lost; it was thought to be possibly in Greenland. It would be almost three hundred years before the American writer and Arctic explorer Charles Francis Hall, sidetracked on Baffin Island while en route to Hudson Bay to search for survivors of the lost Franklin expedition, fortuitously rediscovered Frobisher's sites and his 'straight' and restored them to the maps and history. But Hall not only set the maps to right, he also collected the first oral history among the Inuit. He wrote up in his notebooks interviews with some twenty-five people, among them Ookijoky Ninoo, from whom Lucassie Nowdlak and Inookie Adamie are descended (Inookie is called after Ookijoky Ninoo but says, 'I do not use the name – it is too long'). From the stories Hall heard from Ookijoky and others, he came to believe that Frobisher's lost men had survived in Inuit hands and eventually made a getaway in a boat they built themselves. But Hall's interviews are subject to a variety of interpretations, and Hall may have become committed to his opinion because of his hope and belief that at least some of Franklin's men were alive and living among the Inuit. This was the motivation for his jour-

The Shaman Seeks an Answer, by Mark Emerak (1901–83). Stencil by Mona Ohov-eluk Kuneyuna, 1987, Holman. George Best, one of Frobisher's captains on his second and third voyages, observed *qilaniq* – the practice of divination by head lifting – and wrote in his account of his voyages: 'These people are great enchanters and use manye charmes of Witchcraft. For when their heads do ake, they tye a great stone with a string unto a sticke, and with certain prayers & wordes done to the sticke, they lifte up the stone from the ground, which some-times with all a man's force they cannot stir. & sometimes againe they lifte as easily as a feather, and hope thereby with certain ceremonious words to have ease and help.'

ney. When I ask Inookie what he thinks became of Frobisher's lost men, his reply is unambiguous: 'I am sure the Inuit killed them' (see Appendix 2).

Into his seventies, Inookie Adamie is still a busy walrus hunter and spends much of his time at Torngait – 'spirits' – the camp down the bay his grandparents' parents started. At home in Iqaluit, he likes looking at the book that archaeologists he helped with excavations on Kodlu-narn Island have sent him. The book has a picture of the skirmish at Bloody Point between Inuit and qallunaat. 'Each wanted to be superior,' he says. 'They didn't welcome each other too well. They saw each other for the first time, and they were not sure how to treat each other. Right now if I were to meet someone I've never met before of a different nationality, I wouldn't know what to do or say. In the early days of contact, it would have been very strange and scary, so I can probably understand what the Inuit did. From what I see in the pictures there was probably strong conflict.' And he adds: 'They got to like each other better as they got to know each other better.'

What neither Inuit nor qallunaat knew in 1576 when Frobisher fired his warning shots down Frobisher Bay was that these were merely the opening salvos in the search for a waterway across Arctic America. There would be many passages, but the search would end only in the twentieth century.

1 Into the Arctic Archipelago: Edward Parry in Igloolik and the Shaman's Curse

 The colours of the Arctic today are blue and dove grey, like a Toni Onley watercolour, and on this brilliant clean morning John MacDonald, director of the Igloolik Research Centre, is driving us over the road that leads to the point off which William Edward Parry of the Royal Navy – whom Inuit call Paarii – anchored his expedition in the winter of 1822–3.

Vehicles pass us at speed – they are three- or four–wheel all-terrain vehicles on their way to a summer tent colony at Igloolik Point, where hunters and their families – perhaps a hundred people – are camped for the walrus hunting, a resource as sustaining today as it was during Parry's visit. Large herds, he wrote on the day he drew within sight of Igloolik, 'were lying with their young on almost every loose piece of ice we saw.'[1]

The route we follow has many *inuksuit* – but not very old ones. 'They were probably built by people whose ATVs broke down,' says Carolyn MacDonald. 'They built them while they waited for the repairs.' But there are better antiquities up ahead. 'We're going to visit Mr Elder,' says John MacDonald. In fact, five of us, John and Carolyn, their daughter Lucy, myself, and Claudio Aporta, at the time of my visit an Argentine PhD candidate writing his thesis on the Global Positioning System as used now by Inuit hunters along with age-old navigation techniques, are going to picnic at Mr Elder's grave.

After a while, we stop at a circle of tumbled stones just off the road. They and a tombstone, which juts out of the centre, are encrusted with golden and crimson lichen. The words on the tombstone read:

Mr. Alexander Elder
Greenland Mate
HBM
Ship Hecla
Obit April 15, 1823
Aged 36 years

The shade of Mr Elder cannot have had an easy time of it. He was buried here, near where Parry's observatory stood, having died, wrote Parry, from 'confirmed dropsy which having attacked the region of the heart, rapidly terminated his existence.'[2] But the late Igloolik elder Mark Ijjangiaq left another version of his end: 'That man's death was caused by a shaman. It had something to do with a thing that someone wanted from him. One of the higher officials refused the request. Of course, they were low on their supplies and had to turn the request down. But that man wanted the thing so badly that with the help of his shaman's powers he killed that white man. That is what I have heard.'[3]

After the burial there was plenty more to prevent the corpse resting in peace. Animals dug up the bones, and for a time, until they decided it was futile, Inuit buried them again,[4] but it was not Mr Elder's ghost that walked, it was the headstone. It was discovered across Baffin Island in a whalers' graveyard near Pond Inlet by the Oblate missionary and archaeologist Father Guy-Mary Rousseliere. The priest repatriated it in 1948, when he took up parish duties for a time in Igloolik, 125 years after Mr Elder's burial.

So it is not at all certain that the headstone stands today exactly in its original position. But from where we picnic, we would have viewed, in the winter of 1822–3, the *Fury* and the *Hecla* in the bay before us, the *Hecla* under second-in-command, George F. Lyon, to the distant side of the bay – though close enough that a rope stretched over snow blocks, as Lyon shows in his sketch, could guide personnel between the vessels in the Arctic winter; and before us, one cable length from shore, the *Fury*, under Parry, expedition commander.

The *Fury* and the *Hecla* were the first ships ever to reach Igloolik. No more would come for a hundred years, and this isolation too was the shaman's revenge. I learn the reason why from Rosie Iqallijuq, Igloolik's most senior citizen.[5] 'When the two ships were leaving, they were cursed by a shaman never to return. Naturally the crew of the ships had been getting girlfriends – no wonder, they were men! Perhaps the Inuit men were jealous types. One of the wives who got involved with a crew

Parry's Farthest, attained on his first voyage into the Arctic archipelago during 1819–20. The sketch shows HMS *Griper* off the west end of Melville Island. (HMS *Hecla* is round the point, a few miles to the west.) No one would sail further west for thirty years. Watercolour over pencil on wove paper. By Midshipman Andrew Motz Skene (1796–1849), 1820. From an unpublished sketchbook begun while the artist was on the British naval voyage taking Napoleon to exile on the island of St Helena.

member was the wife of the shaman Qimmungat and he – the shaman – "suvijavininga" – he blew the ship away! From that day on, no ship arrived. The curse of the shaman persisted for a long long time and so no ships were able to make it to this area.'

The Start of Nineteenth-Century Arctic Exploration

When Parry anchored off Igloolik, he was thirty-two and already well on the way to his unchallenged position as Britain's towering figure in nineteenth-century Arctic exploration. Deeply religious, diligent but daring, his rapid rise to prominence began after he captained the *Alexander* on the British Navy's first nineteenth-century attempt to reach the Pacific from the Atlantic via a Northwest Passage. This was the 1818 expedition under command of the dogmatic, brave – he proved it again and again – but always controversial Captain John Ross.

Some 250 years after Frobisher, the British Admiralty had decided to energetically pursue a program of Arctic exploration. In the aftermath of the Napoleonic wars, a window of opportunity had opened up: vessels and men were freed up with the peace and needed employment, and climate conditions were propitious. Whalers reported open water in high latitudes and a remarkable melting of icefields. And most important, eager to seize the moment, was the second secretary of the Admiralty, John – later, Sir John – Barrow, who would be the chief proponent and great facilitator of African, Arctic, and Antarctic exploration during the first half of the nineteenth century.[6] Barrow now 'stongly urged the necessity of accomplishing that discovery to which our old navigtors had led the way,' wrote Parry's son, the Rev. Edward Parry, in his memoir of his father's life.[7] And supporting the Admiralty's decision was a groundswell of popular enthusiasm.

As a result of these circumstances, in 1818 four vessels were fitted out, two to explore from the Sea of Spitsbergen towards the North Pole in pursuit of a direct route across the pole, a theory that had its adherents and would die hard, and two for the search for a Northwest Passage.

At the time, it was known that above continental North America a polar sea existed. With the formation of the Hudson's Bay Company in 1670, fur traders had begun to explore the northern lands. In 1771, Samuel Hearne attained the mouth of the Coppermine; in 1789, Alexander Mackenzie reached the mouth of the Mackenzie. And exploring from the Pacific in 1778, Captain James Cook rounded present-day Alaska and reached Icy Cape. But the geography of the Arctic Sea and its fractured land masses was unknown. The Northwest Passage was still to be discovered.

This task went first to John Ross, forty years old, irritatingly opinionated, but an excellent seaman with a great deal of experience and good connections. The Admiralty charged him with 'exploring Baffin's Bay and inquiring into the probability of a North-West Passage.' His instructions were informative: 'It appears that a current of some force runs from northward towards the upper part of Davis Strait, during the summer season, bringing with it fields of ice in the spring, and ice bergs in the summer ... there would, therefore seem reason to suppose, that it may be derived from an open sea, in which case, Baffin's Bay cannot be bounded by land, as our charts generally represent it, but must communicate with the Arctic Ocean.'[8] The Admiralty was optimistic he might reach Kamchatka and provided instructions about what to do if he did.

Ross sailed on his flagship the *Isabella*, a hired whaler, in company with the *Alexander*, captained by second-in-command, Lt William Edward Parry, already a Barrow favourite.[9] Ross had aboard as interpreter a Greenland Christian Eskimo, John Sackheouse, probably the first Eskimo artist whose name we know. Ross took his expedition far north up the west coast of Greenland, where high on the coast he met uncontacted Eskimo. They had never before seen white people. 'Wild people,' declared John Sackheouse. To them the *Isabella* and the *Alexander* seemed animate beings. Pointing to the ships, they asked, wrote John Ross, 'What creatures were they?' To which Sackheouse replied that they 'were houses made of wood.' This they seemed to discredit, answering, 'No. They are alive, we have seen them move their wings.'[10] This was the kind of natural history story the British public liked to hear, but the Ross expedition would be a resounding disappointment.

Ross lingered a few days with the 'wild people,' whom he called the Arctic Highlanders (today known as the Polar Eskimo or, scientifically, the Inuhuit) and then rounded Baffin Bay, sailing northwest past what the maps called Smith Sound – he did not detect that the sound was a strait and that the waters made Greenland an island. He continued down past Jones Sound – in fact, another waterway – and arrived in the waters of so-called Lancaster Sound. Ross would not easily repair the damage done his reputation when, in the very face of success, he decided (wrongly) that no entrance to the west existed through what was, in fact, Lancaster Strait.

On 30 August 1818 on the *Alexander* behind the *Isabella*, Lt William Edward Parry wrote, 'Here Baffin's hopes of passage began to be less, every day more than another; here on the contrary, mine grow strong. I think there is something in his account which gives cause to suspect he did not see the bottom of Lancaster Sound.'[11]

The next day, the *Isabella* tacked and retreated. John Ross believed the way forward to be blocked by a range of mountains – he called them the Crocker Mountains (a mirage).

On both vessels there were officers who strongly disagreed with the decision, Parry among them. Back in England, officers wrote to the press. Parry expressed his feelings in a letter home. 'You must know that, on our late voyage, we entered a magnificent strait from thirty to sixty miles wide upon the west coast of Baffin's Bay, and – came out again, nobody knows why!' Of the likelihood of a Northwest Passage, he wrote, 'I know it is in existence and not very hard to find.'[12]

He was wrong; the search would be long and hard and cost many lives.

Parry's Farthest

After Ross's failure to discover that Lancaster Sound was a Strait, the Admiralty listened to the dissent that was soon in the public arena and readied a new expedition. They gave the command to Barrow's favourite, William Edward Parry, and, still a lieutenant but in command of his own expedition, Parry made his most revolutionary voyage: he sailed through Lancaster Strait, across the Arctic archipelago, and wintered triumphantly with the *Hecla* and the *Griper* far to the west in Winter Harbour at Melville Island (which he named after the first Lord of the Admiralty). Ice blocked his further progress – no one would sail further west for thirty years – but Parry knew he had discovered that a sea route existed from Baffin Bay to the Pacific. 'Of the existence of such a passage, and that the outlet will be found at Bering Strait, it is scarcely possible, on an inspection of the map, with the addition of our discoveries and in conjunction with those of Cook and Mackenzie, any longer to entertain a reasonable doubt.'[13]

Parry returned to London to find that fame and the news of his triumph had preceded him by several hours. A bachelor still, his romances were followed by all of society. He had, in fact, explored one of the several routes by which a Northwest Passage can be accomplished. But the heavy pack ice he encountered had made him believe there was likely to be a more southerly, superior passage.

It was the search for this passage, which he rightly thought would lie close to the coast of continental America, that now brought Com-

Portrait of Edward Parry, drawn during Parry's 1821–3 expedition. The word 'Captain' at the left was added by the collector George F. Lyon, who brought the drawing back to England.

mander Parry (he would soon be promoted to Captain) in the years 1821–3 through Hudson Strait and the Bay on a voyage during which he would winter twice in the ice, the second time off Igloolik Island. Igloolik lies at the eastern end of what is now the Fury and Hecla Strait. This ice-choked strait separates the north shore of Melville Peninsula from Baffin Island. It would not provide the route he sought – it would take Canadian icebreakers to make the Fury and Hecla Strait readily navigable – and later, in a private letter Parry described his expedition as 'unsuccessful, but, I trust & believe, not discreditable.'[14] In fact, the records he and second-in-command, twenty-five-year-old George F. Lyon, kept and published of their close contact with native people would supply for many years to come the best accounts of Inuit life. These accounts, with their geographic and ethnographic data, endure as classic texts of exploration.

But Igloolik Inuit now have their own exceptionally well-filed, well-shelved historical record. Since 1986 when the first interviews were recorded, many of the contributors have died, but their stories are alive and readily accessible through the archives of the Inullariit Elders' Society in the Igloolik Research Centre. They grow more valuable year by year.

Paarii in Igloolik, as Inuit Tell It

As soon as possible after I arrive in Igloolik, I go with interpreter Leah Otak to visit Rosie Iqallijuq, the community's foremost authority on Paarii and his times. (We are only just in time, for, sadly, Rosie died in 2000.) We find her sitting on her bed amid contemporary futons and pillows, her television on in the background. On her wall is a memento from her past – an Inuit broom made from a beautiful white goose wing. 'I know of explorers from what I have heard,' she says. 'It is a long time ago that Igloolik first saw a ship.'

I am anxious to pursue the story of the shaman's curse, its origins and outcome – but, to begin with, from the Inuit point of view, why did Parry come to Igloolik in the first place? From her own elders, the famous Ataguttaaluk and her husband, Ituksarjuat, whom southerners called the King and Queen of Igloolik, Rosie learned a version of the ancient Inuit creation myth that links Parry's arrival with the coming into existence of the Inuit, white people, and Indians (who traditionally were enemies).

'There once was a girl called Uinigumasuittuq who was married to

Parry's vessels at Igloolik. Parry anchored at what he called Turton Bay, but which Inuit called Ikpiarjuq, meaning 'raised beaches.' This was off Ungaluujat, so named because of a nearby large stone circle where Inuit held celebrations when a whale was captured. Here, Parry's vessel the *Fury* is in the foreground, and the *Hecla*, to the distant side of the bay. A rope over snow blocks, as second-in-command George F. Lyon shows in his picture, guided crews between the vessels.

her dog. Because she was married to her dog, her father got bothered in his sleep. So he took his daughter to the island of Qikiqtaarjuk, so she could have her husband with her there. She gave birth to six babies – two were Inuit, two were intimidating half-Indian half-dogs, and two were half-white half-dogs. The father brought the half-Indian half-dogs over to the mainland, and it is said that is why there are unapproachable people there – because of the dogs the father took to the mainland.

'The two half-white half-dog babies were put into the sole of a kamik with two stems of grass and let go into the ocean. Then all of a sudden there was fog; there were bells ringing in the air, and the father could see a mast from the grasses, and sails of a boat like the sails of the boat in which Paarii came. You could see this boot sole, with the two babies in it, leaving the shore. There were only the two babies in the boot sole – a girl and a boy – but that's how the white people multiplied; they had children from one another. Uinigumasuittuq created the white people – these two children who had so many babies. Paarii and his people came around here for the skull of their mother and took it from Qikiqtaarjuk – but we didn't see that![15]

Rosie says all these events happened in the years 'when Qikiqtaarjuk was an island still.' In fact, only in the relatively recent past, perhaps four hundred years ago, as a result of isostatic rebound, did Qikiqtaarjuk become joined to Igloolik and become an isthmus. However, Parry's maps show Qikiqtaarjuk attached to Igloolik Island by a narrow neck of land; since Parry's time, estimates suggest the land has risen a metre and a half.

John MacDonald, who often used to visit Rosie to listen to her stories, makes the case that to the Inuit of Parry's day this creation story made good sense. 'White men had never appeared around Igloolik before. People must have wondered why they were there; the nature of their mission was difficult to comprehend. Given Parry's interest in the island and obsession with the bones he found lying around, what better interpretation could there be?' For Parry and his crews did take away skulls.

We learn about this in Parry's journal entry for 23 July, when shortly after his arrival in Igloolik he goes to visit an abandoned Inuit winter camp. 'In every direction around the huts were lying innumerable bones of walruses and seals, together with the skulls of dogs, bears, and foxes ... We were not a little surprised to find also a number of human skulls lying about among the rest, within a few yards of the huts; and were somewhat inclined to be out of humour on this account with our new friends, who not only treated the matter with the utmost indifference, but on observing that we were inclined to add some of them to our collections, went eagerly about to look for them, and tumbled, perhaps, the craniums of some of their own relations, into our bag ...'[16]

Inuit today will tell you that before the missionaries came they didn't put their dead in boxes – indeed, they had no wood. 'We put rocks around the body and eventually the animals scattered the bones.' And for a long time there were elders who asked to be buried in the old Inuit way. 'Some people feared the priests' burial – they feared their spirits would be caught by the weight of the rocks on top of them.'[17]

Rosie heard many more of her stories from Ulluriaq, a potent personality of the past with whom she once shared the igloo. Ulluriaq lived to a great age and, according to local tradition, was a child herself when Paarii came to Igloolik. Her name means 'star,' and people say she used to summon the power of the stars with her shaman spirit.[18] The young Cambridge graduate Graham Rowley met Ulluriaq during the British-Canadian 1936–9 Arctic expedition led by Tom Manning, and while in his book *Cold Comfort* he didn't commit himself on Ulluriaq's age, he wrote: 'Her father and mother, or perhaps it had been an uncle or an aunt, were said to have met Parry and Lyon during the winter of 1822–23 and all the old men remembered her as having been an old woman when they were boys. One man said ... "Even the land has grown up since she was a girl" ... she remembered when the sea came up to the igloo where her parents had lived. It had been a site that was now half a mile inland.'[19]

Rosie met Ulluriaq when she was about thirteen, after she had travelled by dog team from Chesterfield Inlet to begin her arranged marriage to an older man. 'I first saw Ulluriaq when I got to this area. She was already very old – handicapped by old age – and was sharing the abode with us. I was married to Amaroalik, an old man, very much older than me. Ulluriaq used to tell me stories of the shamans, stories of the explorers. It was basically to put a smile on your face ...

'Ulluriaq told of the time when the ship first arrived – Paarii and his group. Ulluriaq's family were living in Pinngiqalik – Pinger Point- and the ship was travelling towards Igloolik. The hunters got on their kayaks, taking some women with them, and followed the ship, and when it anchored the kayaks went down to the anchored ship.'

Describing this same event, on 16 July 1822, Parry wrote: 'At thirty minutes past nine A.M. we observed several tents on the low shore immediately abreast of us, and presently afterwards five canoes made their appearance at the edge of the land-ice intervening between us and the beach. As soon therefore as we had satisfactorily made out the position and state of the ice, I left the *Fury* in a boat, accompanied by some of the officers, and being joined by Captain Lyon went to meet the Esquimaux.'[20]

Says Rosie, 'It was then that the community of Igloolik was first established. They wintered at Ungaluujat, past Igloolik Point. You can see the camp grounds today, and you can see that it was a very well-established camp.'

There were always Inuit camps – and there still are seasonal Inuit camps – at Igloolik Point, but Parry anchored five miles away in what he called Turton Bay (Inuit call the bay Ikpiarjuq – 'raised beaches') off Ungaluujat, a word that gets its meaning from a large stone circle nearby where Inuit held celebrations when a whale was captured. On this point near Parry's anchorage, the expedition set up tents. Quite soon Inuit began to visit and camp out, building their own sod houses, and sometimes using old Thule houses.[21]

Qallunaat Gifts

When the Inuit first met the white men, Rosie says, their goods initially seemed useless. 'Apparently Inuit received some tobacco from the ship and at that time the tobacco came in the form of squares which had to be cut into small pieces – and apparently Ulluriaq started using these tobaccos as her toys – they were perfectly square. In those days, they were still living in sealskin tents, and one day it started to rain. As a result, the square chunks of tobacco got wet, and when her parents – whose names I never heard – came into the tent, they started to smell something foul. They wondered what it was. So they went over to where Ulluriaq kept her toys and realized it was those square things. The tobacco had gotten wet and was stinking up the tent. Ulluriaq told her parents, "The smell is coming from my pretend blocks." Her father collected all the square tobaccos and threw them away. Smoking tobacco was far from their minds.'

Foodstuffs were similar puzzles. 'When the ice broke up and the ships were leaving, Ulluriaq's parents received sacks of flour, and at that time flour came in large bags. They also received tea, sugar, and biscuits from the ship. Actually what the ship gave away was surplus – what the crew realized they would not be needing on their way home to Europe. And not realizing that biscuits were made for eating, Ul-

Iuriaq and other children started tossing them back and forth. And the sacks of flour were also discarded. When the children realized when you hit the sack it would appear to smoke, they had themselves a time hitting the flour sacks.They hadn't a clue about flour or biscuits – they dare not cook them or eat them, because they didn't know they were food in the first place.'

In Parry's account, flour was carried in barrels; but was flour perhaps sometimes distributed in bags? Or is this an instance of blended oral history, a later story now contributing to Rosie's account of Parry's largesse, but which perhaps originally related to supplies received from other sources, possibly the whalers, and heard by Rosie during her childhood at Chesterfield Inlet on the Hudson Bay coast?

Certain things were rapidly integrated into the culture. 'At that time,' says Rosie, 'they started drinking tea and using sugar. And what they appreciated was ammunition. It was used and very much appreciated.'

Parry's expedition left only one gun behind. He rewarded an Inuk helper Toolema, with a 'rifle-gun,' he wrote in his *Journal of a Second Voyage for the Discovery of a North-West Passage*, '... together with a sufficient quantity of ammunition to last him one summer, after which the gun would probably become useless itself for want of cleaning. It was astonishing to see the readiness with which these people learned to fire at a mark, and the tact they displayed in everything relating to this art. Boys from twelve to sixteen years of age would fire a fowling-piece, for the first time, with perfect steadiness; and the men, with very little practice, would soon become superior marksmen. As, however, the advantage they could derive from the use of firearms must be of very short duration [from lack of ammunition], and the danger to any careless individuals very considerable, we did not, on any other occasion consider it prudent to furnish them in this manner.'[22]

And suddenly all the women were resplendent with beads. 'They liked the beads so much they started beading and used them for bracelets. The first beads they received were not the best quality, I've heard, but the Inuit liked them so much they started trading for them with sealskins. The quality got better later on in time. I've heard that those who received beads for the first time – when the first white man wintered here – made bracelets from the beads.'

In fact, at the time of Parry's visit, beads were not unknown. Parry wrote that he found beads already in use among Igloolik women. Like other goods, beads spread through inter-Inuit trade. Trade beads came to Canada with the first explorers. In the mid-fifteenth century, the discovery and exploration of Africa gave tremendous impetus to bead manufacturing in Venice, and on nearby Murano and other small islands, the early glass houses shrouded bead-making operations with the greatest secrecy. Merchants and explorers took beads with them as objects of trade, and when the first Europeans entered the Gulf of St Lawrence, Venetian beads – the same as those traded in Africa – arrived in their vessels. The Hudson's Bay Company established its first post at Churchill on the west coast of the Bay in 1685 and intermittently in the next century sent sloops up the coast to trade for oil, whalebone, and ivory. In all probability, on board were glass seed trade beads and supplies of the Cornaline d'Aleppo, a tubular bead of red glass wound on an opaque white, transparent green, or yellow core, which became known as the Hudson's Bay bead because the company distributed them everywhere. Igloolik Inuit may also have begun to receive beads from the whalers, who just a few years earlier, in 1817, had begun operating high off the east Baffin coast. But the expedition's presence made beads abundant. 'Many of the [women], in the course of the second winter, covered the whole front of their jackets with the beads they received from us.'[23]

Of course, the Inuit women also made themselves beautiful with tattoos. George F. Lyon, who provided so much of the expedition's excellent graphic record, made quite an intensive study. In fact, he had himself tattooed: 'She took a piece of caribou sinew, which she blackened with soot. She began the work by sewing a rather deep but short stitch in my skin. When the thread was drawn beneath the skin, she pressed her thumb on the spot so as to press in the pigment ... The work went slowly ... When she had sewed forty stitches and the strip was about two inches long, I felt it was enough.' Lyon's skin was then rubbed with whale oil. He said he could vividly imagine the discomfort a young woman had to endure for beauty's sake.[24]

In her studies of bead-decorated parkas, which became an art form, art historian Bernadette Driscoll has noted that alternating dark and light colour bars in beaded fringes, as well as repetitive geometric motifs, relate to the ancient practice of tattooing.[25]

Why the Curse Was Laid

Despite some squeamishness about Inuit burial practices, relations between the visitors and the Inuit during their winter of residence were

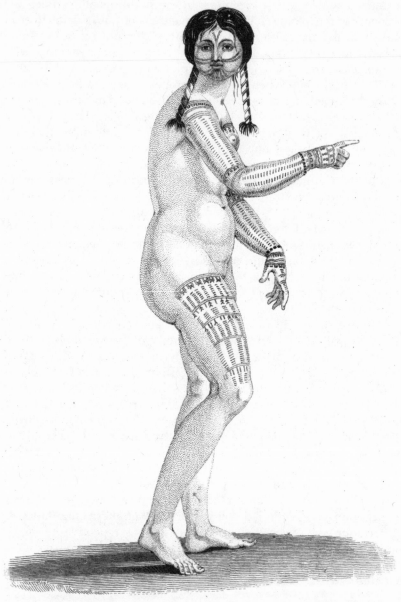

The Manner in Which the Esquimaux Women Are Tattooed. Drawn by George Lyon, 1822–3.

Beaded Amautik. Many women 'covered the whole front of their jackets with the beads they received from us,' wrote Parry in his account of his winter in Igloolik in 1822–3. The artist, Germaine Arnaktauyok, is the niece of the Igloolik storyteller Rosie Iqallijuq, who died in 2000. Pencil crayon.

harmonious. By the time the expedition left, it had altered the Inuit material culture – and possibly the gene pool. The expedition had been peacefully received – its presence useful to the Inuit, and the Inuit helpful to the expedition. The Inuit wanted to trade and were eager to barter, though the white men often gave freely without expecting return. The Inuit had drawn maps, repaired and sewn clothes, and on occasion hospitably hosted officers and crews in their sod houses and tents. Parry had tended the Inuit sick, had set up a makeshift hospital, and shortly before the *Fury* and the *Hecla* began their journey home, he left sledges, wood for bows and arrows, and many useful items for Inuit use, spreading them out around Igloolik in a variety of places, so that as many as possible would benefit. Before departure, as per Admiralty instructions, he set up a flagstaff at a site on the Melville Peninsula, which almost certainly did not stand long. 'The wealth of materials invested in the site – wood, metal, canvas and rope – must have been too valuable an asset for reasonable Inuit to leave intact,' says John Mac-Donald in an article on Parry's flagstaff. 'They may well have considered the mast a final, though curious, parting gift from Parry ... Parry may even have been amused that this significant windfall for his Inuit friends proceeded directly from Admiralty instructions.'[26]

But unfortunately, towards the end of the expedition's stay, harmonious relations were disrupted – a missing shovel brought forth the qallunaat's wrath.

'On the 3d of March [1823],' wrote Parry, 'the Esquimaux were excluded from the *Fury* for some hours, on account of a shovel having been stolen from alongside the preceding day. Soon after this, Oo-ootook, a middle-aged man, who had seldom visited the ships, was in Mr. Skeoch's cabin, when that gentleman explained to him the reason of his countrymen being refused admittance; upon this he became much agitated, trembled exceedingly, and complained of being cold. There could be no doubt he thought Mr. Skeoch had dived into his thoughts; for hastening upon deck, he was a minute or two afterwards detected in bringing back the lost shovel from the place where he had buried it behind our wall. A day or two before this occurrence, Captain Lyon had in a manner somewhat similar recovered a knife that had been stolen from him, for which, by way of punishment, the offender was consigned to solitary confinement for some hours in the Hecla's coal-hole. As, however, the Esquimaux only laughed at this as a very good joke, and as the time was shortly coming when numerous loose stores must be exposed upon the ice near the ships, I determined to make use of the present well-authenticated instance of theft, in trying the effect of some more serious penalty.'

Parry administered naval discipline: 'The delinquent was therefore put down into the Fury's store-room passage, and closely confined there for several hours; when having collected several of the natives on board the Fury, I ordered him to be stripped and seized up in their presence, and to receive a dozen lashes on the back with a cat-o'-nine tails. The instant this was over, his countrymen called out very earnestly, "Timun, timunna," (That's right, that's right,) and seemed much relieved from the fright they had before been in while the fate of the thief seemed doubtful; but in three minutes after not one of them was to be found near the ships, for they hurried off to the huts as fast as their legs and sledges could carry them. This example proved just what we desired; in less than eight-and-forty hours, men, women, and children came to the ships with the same confidence as before, always abusing Oo-oo-took, pronouncing themselves and us uncommonly good people, but evidently more cautious than before of really incurring our displeasure.'[27]

But according to the stories told today, the Inuit were not as pleased about this retribution as Parry appears to have thought. 'Taima, taima' can be interpreted as 'the end,' the end, or 'enough, enough.' When the story was told, more than forty years later, to Charles Francis Hall, who was collecting oral history from the Inuit while on his search for survivors of the lost Franklin expedition, the thief had become a heroic victim.

Hall heard his version[28] from a woman called Erktua, who had visited Parry and Lyon's ships: 'Oo-oo-took, a superior an-nat-ko was charged by Parry when at Ig-loo-lik with the crime of theft for taking a shovel ... Then Parry caused him to be whipped with something that was made of ropes with knots in them – cat-o'-nine-tails. The Innuits standing around and witnessing all this wanted to help Oo-oo-took defend himself, but he said: "Let the Kob-lu-nas try to kill me; they cannot, for I am an an-nat-ko." Then Oo-oo-took's hands were untied, after which the kob-lu-nas tried to cut his head and hands off with long knives – probably swords. Every time a blow was struck, the extreme end of the knife came close to Oo-oo-took's throat; occasionally the blade came just above the crown of his head, and when the attempt was made to cut off his hands the long knife came down very near his wrists; but, after all, he was uninjured because he was a very good An-nat-ko.'

After the flogging, the shaman was confined below decks: 'After Oo-

oo-took had been one day and one night in the dark hole, he thought he would use his power as an an-nat-ko, and destroy the vessel by splitting it through the middle from stem to stern. So he commenced calling to his aid the Good Spirit, when a great cracking noise was made, now and then, under the ship, and at the end of the two days and two nights' confinement, the kob-lu-nas, fearing from such great and terrific noises that the ship would be destroyed, let Oo-oo-took go.'

For generations this story has circulated not only in Igloolik but all along the Arctic ocean coast, sometimes melded with stories of other expeditions, and certainly with additional colourful elements. In the versions people tell today, sometimes the theft of the shovel is mentioned; sometimes it isn't.

Lena Kingmiatook of Taloyoak, tells a particularly full and dramatic version. This was interpreted and sometimes augmented by legal interpreter Tommy Anguttitauruq: 'These white people took an Inuk prisoner whose name was Eqilaglu. This little man was also a shaman and the reason he became a prisoner was because he didn't want his wife to be abused by these white people. He was probably trying to protect his wife. These authorities took him and tied him upside down to a mast so he would agree that these white people could do whatever they wanted to do to his wife. That's why they captured him and treated him very roughly. They had a big axe and they tried to kill him, but since he was such a powerful shaman the axe would go right through him and just cut the wooden pole. No marks on him!

'The little man had a tent made of sealskin probably – not cotton as we have today, for sure. Every time they tried to kill him, every time they swung the axe, other Inuit watching could see him walking into his tent, his spirit going to his tent. He was a shaman and a very stout little person; he didn't want his wife to be taken by these white people. He probably tried to do something that was not pleasant to these white people since they wanted to freely help themselves. At that time we didn't have the rifles or guns or weapons that the white people had. All we had were harpoons, spears, and knives made of bones. So although there were some Inuit there watching, they were not helping him. The white men tortured him, tried to kill him with an axe, and hung him upside down so the blood would go up to his head and he would go crazy and be unable to use his power.

'The little shaman was very helpless. He didn't want to give up his wife and also his steel snow knife, but he didn't have enough power. The other Inuit people know he is asking for help. All the shamans get together and they mumble and mumble in a low, low voice and it sounds like thunder roaring in the tent. It was a prayer to bring help to the little man. He began getting more power from the other shamans; that way he got harder and harder to kill.

'Even though he was tied up, as soon as people looked away from him, he'd completely disappear and walk right into his tent. Each time, someone would bring him back, and tie him up, and try to kill him again. The ice was breaking up and they tried to get him to agree they should take his wife along. But he wouldn't agree and the ship stayed there even though the ship could travel now. Then the captain told them: "Now it's up to me. We leave this man alone now and give him back his wife. We cannot do anything more because we do not have his power."

'They brought Eqilaglu back to his tent and gave him back his wife. And they began to rush, rush, getting ready to leave at a certain time of day. But the little man said to himself, "That ship, those white people, have treated me so badly." Then the little man said a certain word "Pamiuluq!" That's old language. Pamiuluq is a spirit with a bad tail. The little man said, "Pamiuluq will chew up their ship." That's what he said, looking at the ship. "The white people treated me so badly so Pamiuluq will chew up their ship."'

Herve Paniaq of Igloolik gives a horrific account of the shaman's sufferings and subsequent action: 'He had stolen a shovel so he was taken. He was made to lie on his back on deck with his hands tied. The white people wanted to axe off his arms ... He was made to lie on his back, but his arm could not be axed. When they tried to axe his arm, it looked as if his arm was severed, so much so that the blade would stick fast to the deck, but each time his arm was untouched. After numerous attempts had been made, they gave it up. When they were done with him, he blew them away and told them never to return again. As the ship had spent a good deal of time in the region, they kept wanting to return but it was no longer possible.'[29]

Pauli Kunnuk also recorded his version of how the shaman took revenge: 'I've heard a bit about Paarii ... [and] the time the white people stayed down at Ungaluujat. An Inuk had stolen a shovel. It is said that the white person really got mad over the incident, which is understandable because of the theft. Because of the way the man got mad over it, the Inuk made it not possible for ships ever to return on account of the ice. That's what I heard, whether there is any truth in it or not I cannot say. But it is said that through shamanism it was no longer possible for

ships to make it here. Certainly without a doubt, shamanism was practised in those times.'[30]

After Paarii wintered, for more than a hundred years, no vessel came
to Igloolik. This was the shaman's curse.

The Lifting of the Curse

As a small boy in the early 1900s, Mark Ijjangiaq believed white men
were rare. 'I thought there were only a few worldwide.' When for the
first time he visited Pond Inlet on the east coast of Baffin Island, where
southern vessels harboured, he found 'there were a few white people,
but what I did not realize was there were many, many more where they
came from. I thought Inuit were numerous in comparison – because I
knew there were a lot of them.'[31]

In fact, by the early 1900s, Inuit in certain areas of the Canadian Arctic had had contact – often close – with qallunaat for three-quarters of a
century. The whalers *Elizabeth* and *Larkins* out of British ports, which
appeared high off Baffin Island's northeast coast five years before Parry
wintered at Igloolik, were harbingers of many more. In pursuit of the
bowhead, Scottish and English vessels whaled in numbers down the
east Baffin coast and eventually into the whale-rich waters of Cumberland Sound. Here, Americans joined the chase; they introduced wintering and set up shore stations, and then in the 1860s their vessels sailed
into Hudson Bay and the great whaling theatre of Roes Welcome
Sound. In the whaling areas, the Inuit soon became necessary partners
in the North's first industry. Inuit in these areas now had access to the
white man's goods, which soon were indispensable. When whaling
declined and the whalers took their leave, for the most part before the
First World War, the traders, in pursuit of white fox furs (sometimes
recycled whalers, later the personnel of the Hudson's Bay Company),
were there to take their place. They set up permanent trading posts, and
for practicality in these remote locations eventually the missions and
sometimes the Royal Canadian Mounted Police (originally the Royal
North West Mounted Police) set up shop next door.

But because of ice conditions – and the shaman's curse – Igloolik
Inuit remained profoundly isolated.

Still, the late Noah Piugaattuk, one of Igloolik's greatest storytellers,
related that in his youth there were expectations of change.[32] 'The
rumour circulated that in the future the white man would eventually
arrive in the Igloolik area. Since the white men had started to arrive [in

the Keewatin and Baffin Island areas], they would continue flowing to the North.'

Igloolik has a vigorous tradition about how the curse of the shaman was vanquished.

Aya, I think I have heard –
(He has heard from the wind)
I think I have heard –
(He thinks he has heard)
The sound of wood out in the wild
Aya, Aya, Aya.

Noah Piugaattuk recalls that around the turn of the twentieth century (some consider the song is of earlier origin, even predating Parry) an Igloolik Inuk made up this song for use in a drum dance. The composer, whose name was Imaruittuq, danced with the drum, while his wife and another woman sang his song. In many verses, the song tells those who have gathered in the giant igloo built for celebration, that after years without contact the white man will soon come again to Igloolik. But will he come by water or by land? That was the question. The verses of Imaruittuq's song allow for either possibility – a sled could come out of the wild or a vessel grind through the ice.

I think I have heard
He thinks he has heard from the sea
I believe that I hear
He believes that he hears
The sound of wood from the sea.

'The ships in those days only sailed, so they were not able to have access to locations that have a lot of ice. The strait that blocks these waters usually has a lot of ice, so it was difficult for ships to pass through in those times when they depended on sail. The question was: what route would the white man take to come to Igloolik? Perhaps he would arrive by land; or would he arrive by sea?' The song that asked the question was sung in the giant igloo when Piugaattuk was a child. 'The song was made long ago, knowing the inevitability of white settlement.'

Igloolik people say the first white man came by land – in 1913, by dog team. They say he was the French-Canadian explorer Alfred Tremblay – whom Inuit call 'Tamali' – who had come north looking for gold.

(In fact, Charles Francis Hall had visited Igloolik on his search for survivors of Sir John Franklin's expedition just forty-four years after Parry. Inuit received him hospitably and told him their stories. They called him 'Mistahoh,' and Rosie made a brief reference to him after Leah and I asked if she had ever heard of him: 'He was here for a while; then he went on towards Hall Beach and on from there.' Rosie expressed the opinion that he was related to a member of the lost Franklin crews. 'That's why he was anxious to find them. White people are much unlike Inuit; when they want to know something, they go to any lengths to find answers to their questions. He was very anxious, as he was related to one of the crew members.')

But, according to Igloolik elders, it was Tremblay who broke the shaman's spell. He had shipped in 1912 with Captain Joseph Bernier, a veteran Arctic mariner, on the *Minnie Maud*, an old fishing schooner hastily fitted out to pursue a rumour of 'a new Eldorado' in North Baffin Island. Gold nuggets were said to have been found in the bed of the Salmon River flowing into Eclipse Sound. Tremblay set off overland with Inuit guides to look for minerals, game, and anything else of interest. He was the first white man to cross the land from the head of Admiralty Sound to Fury and Hecla Strait. He described his journey in his book *Cruise of the Minnie Maud*.

He reached Igloolik on 20 March 1913.[33] 'When morning broke I saw the low lying land of Igloolik Island ahead of me ... we struggled into the native village, at the south-eastern extremity of the island, about noon, and standing on the shore I saw four Eskimos ...' Tremblay had no knowledge that Hall had preceded him. 'These natives were very astonished when they saw me as I was the first white man to visit Igloolik since Sir W.E. Parry, the pioneer and champion explorer of the British Navy, had wintered there with his historic ships the Fury and the Hecla in 1822–23 ... Some of these natives had never seen a white man before and held them in fear. They had heard of Parry and his men only through tradition.' Tremblay and his guides were too exhausted to explain their presence. They slept for twenty-four hours in their host Eetootajoo's igloo. But on 23 March, Tremblay set out to explore Igloolik Island. 'The island resembles the form of a crouching bear with the head towards the east and the tail towards the west.'

Noah Piugaattuk was a little boy when Tremblay arrived. 'I heard him say that Igloolik was like a wild animal, very hard to catch. When animals are alerted and alarmed, they tend to take off. Igloolik was like such an animal, alerted by the white man and captured because Tamali, a white man, had arrived here ... He walked to Igloolik Point and looked at [remains of] the old sod houses there. On his return from his walking journey, he said his exploration had been like capturing an animal – which then becomes available for food. Now people would easily come here and do whatever they needed to do.'[34]

Rosie says Tamali shot up the island. 'It is said that he had a pistol and with it he shot up the island of Igloolik as he walked around the shoreline. Afterwards, he said Igloolik was dead – ships would now be able to get to the island.'

From Igloolik, Tremblay conducted a few further exploratory forays and then returned to the Pond Inlet area, taking with him Parry's ice anchor, today in a Quebec museum. He may also have been involved in the removal of Mr Elder's wandering gravestone (superstition perhaps preventing its journey south on shipboard), but Tremblay's Inuit guide, Nuqallaq, usually gets the credit: it is said he took it along to trade for tobacco. Nuqallaq would gain greater notoriety in a few years' time for the murder of the demented free trader Robert Janes.[35]

Though Tamali had lifted the curse, it would still be two decades before Igloolik saw a ship. The pace of change quickened after the Hudson's Bay Company and the Catholic Oblate Mission arrived at Chesterfield Inlet in 1913, and over the next decades both the church and the white fox fur traders pushed into the high North, establishing missions and trading posts in even the most remote locations on the Arctic ocean coast. But, say Igloolik people, 'Igloolik was the last to have white people.' Only in 1931 did the first ship since the *Fury* and the *Hecla* appear offshore.[36]

The elder Hubert Amarualik recalled for the oral history program the time when he went as a child with his family down past the area where Parry's expedition had set up tents, and camped by the old Inuit sod-house ruins: 'We made camp there to wait for the ship that was to bring the mission building.'[37] At that time, Amarualik said the tent rings made by the Parry expedition were still intact, and people kept themselves busy looking for 'treasure' while they waited for the vessel that would bring the mission. 'It was at that particular time they used to dig, hoping to find something that might have been left by those white people. We used to walk to this place from our tent on many occasions with shovels, because it was said that something had been buried by the white people who wintered there. It first started by someone telling a story. The place where the white people had their camp is very easy to distinguish, so they dug all over the place. Of course, they found nothing.'

Digging in the old Inuit Thule culture sod houses was more productive of items of interest; diggers might come upon Thule artifacts. Rosie says, 'Sometimes we found small combs with long tines – but my hair was too thick! And we used to find beautiful little birds carved with flints. It always amazed me that these beautiful little carvings were made only with flint.'

Why does she think the earlier people made these beautiful little carvings? 'They had their own minds.'

Rosie, who had spent her childhood around Chesterfield Inlet when there were already white people, was there to watch when the ship bringing the wood to Igloolik for the first mission came into view.[38] 'I recognized that boat when it was arriving. It was the *Tiriisikuluk* [the *Theresa*], only a small one. The women who were living in the same camp as me began yelling out "UMIAQJUARAALUUK!! – A huge big ship!" They seemed to have lost their minds. I became scared of these ladies who went crazy over the ship ... but they were only happy because the boat was arriving. I said it was really not such a very big ship. They were amazed!

'Ever since that time, ships have come regularly again. It seems in the past they had been blown away by the shaman.'

2 John Ross at Kablunaaqhiuvik – the 'Place for Meeting White People'

'The wreck gave a lot of wealth to this area in terms of metal. A lot of their relics were used for kudluks or harpoons. Before the shipwreck the Inuit were mostly using bones and antlers for their weapons. Afterwards they used the wood and material that were left behind – and there are a couple of areas around Thom Bay where people still find things today.'

That's Bibian Neeveeovak of Taloyoak telling us with interpreter Louise Anaija about the wreck of John Ross's vessel the *Victory* at Kablunaaqhiuvik – the place for meeting white people – and what it meant to Inuit all over the Boothia Peninsula, and, through inter-Inuit trade, beyond.

Neeveeovak – her baptismal name is rarely used – is the only woman I meet on my visits to the Arctic Ocean coast who has the traditional woman's tattoos on her face. 'They used special bone needles with a trough for natural ink – soot from the lamp mixed with seal oil. Yes, it hurt when the needle went through the skin.' Taloyoak people call Neeveeovak 'the last Netsilik,' the name for the Inuit who once hunted all over the Boothia Peninsula and beyond and had their heartland in the Netsilik Lake area. When I ask what it means when they describe her this way, she says, 'I don't know exactly, but I'm the oldest in Gjoa Haven, Pelly Bay, and here in Taloyoak.'

Last night, Neeveeovak won a split in the community telephone bingo, and while we talk, the Discovery Channel – Nunavut's favourite – plays in the background. But Neeveeovak's memories of the hard traditional life with its tough choices are never far away. 'I was born in

August while my father was away catching fall-run fish, waiting at a river for the caribou to cross. A shaman at my birth gave me the name Neeveeovak – "housefly" – so that I would have easy access to food – like a housefly. When my father returned, he came home empty-handed because the caribou had failed to come. He told my mother I should be put out to freeze. They used to freeze the newborn babies, leaving them out until they died. But my mother had been packing me up on her back for a long time, and so my grandmother refused. That's why I'm alive today. "Igitaujuq" [the putting out of babies to die] stopped only when the RCMP said not to.[1] Perhaps in the old way there was too much maleness, but today a lot of people complain of not having enough of this or that. They complain but they are wealthy compared to how Inuit used to be. The Netsilik people had to use the old covers of their kayaks to make pails and buckets. A lot of people complain but there's a lot of wealth today compared to how it was.

'I'm grateful that the qallunaat ventured up here because their wreck made the Netsilik people survive.'

The wreck of John Ross's *Victory* brought the first suggestion of easy living to the Inuit of the Boothia Peninsula – the last uncontacted Inuit. The wreck was a bonanza with a 'wealth effect' that continued for over one hundred years. Perhaps it's not surprising, considering the benefits, that Inuit are said to tell more stories of the Ross expedition and the *Victory* than they do of any other wrecks or expeditions, including the Franklin tragedy.

John Ross and the *Victory*

Jane Griffin, who would become the second wife of Sir John Franklin and the heroine of Arctic exploration, met John Ross at a dinner party in 1819 at a time when, as a result of his unlucky voyage to Lancaster Sound, controversy and humiliation were settling about him. She wrote in her diary, 'He is short, stout, sailor-looking ... Yet notwithstanding his lack of beauty, he has a great deal of intelligence, benevolence & good humour in his countenance'[2] His great-great-nephew, Rear Admiral M.J. Ross, summed him up in his book *Polar Pioneers* as 'an eccentric, very likeable at times, infuriating at others.'[3] His failure to discover that Lancaster Sound was the sought-after entrance to a Northwest Passage on his 1818 expedition was held against him for years and brought him professional derision – especially following the smashing success of his one-time second-in-command, William Edward Parry. This was not

Victory *Stopped by Ice*.

helped by his bitter relations with the powerful John Barrow, second secretary of the Admiralty. Too rapidly after his return from his 1818 voyage, Ross issued his account of his voyage. 'I have proved the existence of a bay, from Disco to Cumberland Strait, and set to rest for ever the question of a north-west passage ...,' he declared.[4] He was hoist with his own petard. Barrow attacked the report savagely: 'A voyage of discovery implies danger; but a mere voyage like his round the shore of Baffin's Bay, in the three summer months, may be considered as a voyage of pleasure.'[5] This was not a charge anyone would be able to make about John Ross's second voyage in search of the Northwest Passage.

Ross was promoted to Captain after his return – the promotion had probably been in the works – but received no new appointment. (His great-great-nephew believes he may not have put his name forward; however, he was never again employed by the Admiralty.) He retired to his Scottish property on half pay and there was far from idle, devoting himself to the study of steam propulsion, new but already adopted by merchant vessels, writing and preaching its necessary naval use. As usual, it was not in his nature to be tactful. Why were not all naval officers able to see the advantages a steam vessel possessed over a sailing ship, 'so perfectly evident and undeniable'? Answering his own question, he said, 'Officers who are high in rank do not like to look to this apparently uncomfortable mode of warfare and they show a reluctance to study a new system of naval tactics. They cannot easily or willingly abandon the near prospect they have of proudly displaying their flags at the mast-head of a first rate ship of war, one of the most beautiful and splendid objects in the world.'[6] Shortly thereafter, he published a pioneering work in the field,[7] which, though not popular with the Admiralty, went into three editions.[8]

In 1828, Ross decided to put his belief in steam to the most rugged test imaginable. He submitted to the Admiralty a proposal for an attempt by steam vessel on the Northwest Passage. His plan was to take the vessel via Lancaster Sound down Prince Regent's Inlet towards what many naval minds at the time thought would prove an unimpeded route west along the coast of mainland North America. The Admiralty turned him down, but Ross had friends among the well off and the well placed, and the gin manufacturer Felix Booth (his name is found today all over the Arctic map) underwrote the expedition in the amount of £10,000, while Ross himself provided £3,000. He bought the *Victory*, a paddle steamer (originally 85 tons) that had formerly delivered mail, strengthened her hull, and equipped her with new, newly patented paddles, newly patented boilers, and other new machinery. Parry visited the ship and wrote his brother that the expedition was 'bold, and public-spirited' but noted 'there is, in the whole thing, rather too much that is new and untried.'[9] Ross asked the Admiralty for a leave of absence, and the Admiralty showed goodwill, providing a 16-ton decked vessel, which Ross named the *Krusenstern*, for tow behind the *Victory*. (He had also wanted a whaler as an accompanying store ship, but arrangements fell through.) The *Victory* left Britain 13 June 1829, with a complement of four officers, among them Ross's nephew James Clark Ross, who had sailed to the Arctic before, both with his uncle and with Parry, and nineteen men; and equipped with the accoutrements of steam propulsion. These would prove of far greater use to the Inuit than to the expedition.

Ross sailed as planned into Lancaster Sound – 'The spot recals [*sic*] a lively recollection of the various trying emotions of which it has been the parent, and at the same time gives me more than hopes, that the effort which I am once more making to solve the important problem before me may, if I ever return to England, be received in a very different manner.'[10] The engine and paddlewheels proved disappointments even before he left port, but Ross successfully entered Prince Regent's Inlet and visited the spot where in 1825 Parry, on his third and final effort to make the passage, had had to give up and ground the *Fury*. Ross found a great store of abandoned supplies. He took some aboard and continued down the inlet, naming features of the coast en route. At the end of September, he steered into Felix Harbour (named after his patron) and prepared to winter, discarding as soon as possible the engine, from the beginning 'a heavy grievance.' In future, he declared, the *Victory* would be a sailing ship, nothing more.

Arrival of the Inuit

One week into the New Year, the *Victory* received visitors. People all over the Arctic coast – but particularly Inuit in Taloyoak and Pelly Bay – tell the stories of how the Netsilik met qallunaat for the first time at Kablunaaqhiuvik -the 'place for meeting white people.'

'In the time before there were any qallunaat,' says Bibian Neeveeovak, 'a group of hunters happened to be in the Thom Bay area. One hunter wandered away from the group and saw something strange. He went towards it and found the qallunaat. He was scared because he had never seen them before. He ran so fast that the tail of his parka flew out behind him. When he got back home, he told everybody that these were really different people with long necks and long faces. He scared every-one.'

Lena Kingmiatook, Taloyoak's master storyteller, takes up the account: 'Abiluktuq – "long strides" – was seal hunting in the winter-time. There were quite a number of people and it was a very snowy day. Abiluktuq had a dog that was very well trained for smelling out seal holes. Every time the dog smells something, he goes towards the smell. The dog began running and Abiluktuq was running with it, and soon he starts smelling something strange that he has never smelled before. And then he saw something that looked like a mountain, not quite a mountain but so big that he compared it to a mountain, on the ice where he had never seen anything before. Abiluktuq gets closer and sees smoke coming out of the mountain and also people. This man was so scared that he started running with all his might, running away from this strange thing he had just witnessed. He was running so hard and so fast that the tail of his parka was straight out. When Abiluktuq – "long strides" – got home, everyone was scared, not knowing what was in their hunting territory.'[11]

Jose Angutingunirk of Pelly Bay, who can trace his ancestry to his grandfather's father's mother, a baby packed on the back at the time of the Ross expedition, describes what happened next: 'Abiluktuq was the one who saw the masts – and several people walking around – and he told the Inuit hunters, "Just three kilometres from here I saw some masts and people walking around them. I didn't go to them because I was afraid of those masts and what they might do to me." The other hunters got together and started to go to the masts, but then they began to think that the white people might think they were spirits – not peo-ple. "What if they think we're not Inuit – not men?" So they went back home and began their shaman practices. Through his spirit, the shaman spoke to a white man. They spoke in English. Then the shaman told the Inuit the qallunaat were not dangerous and the masts would do no harm to anyone. The next day, they went to the ship.'

John Ross described the encounter from the qallunaat point of view in his journal entry for 9 January 1830: 'Going on shore this morning, one of the seamen informed me that strangers were seen from the ob-servatory. I proceeded accordingly in the direction pointed out, and soon saw four Esquimaux near a small iceberg, not far from the land, and about a mile from the ship. They retreated behind it as soon as they perceived me; but as I approached the whole party came suddenly out of their shelter, forming a body of ten in front and three deep, with one

Abiluktuq – 'long strides' – the first of the Netsilik to see John Ross's *Victory*, was so frightened he ran home as fast as he could with the tail of his parka flying straight out behind him. 'In those days,' says the artist, Germaine Arnaktauyok, 'the man's parka had a long tail.' This famous story is told with much laughter all over the region and sometimes in connection with other expeditions, though Ross makes the provenance clear, as do Pelly Bay elders, whose ancestors visited the ship. Pencil crayon.

man detatched, on the land side, who was apparently sitting on a sled. I therefore sent back my companion for Commander Ross to join me, together with some men, who were directed to keep at a distance behind him ...

'Knowing that the word of salutation between meeting tribes was Tima tima, I hailed them in their own language, and was answered by a general shout of the same kind; the detached man being then called in front of their line. The rest of my party now coming up, we advanced to within sixty yards, and then threw our guns away, with the cry *Aja, Tima*; being the usual method, as we had learned it, of opening a friendly communication. On this, they threw their knives and spears in the air in every direction, returning the shout Aja, and extending their arms to show that they also were without weapons. But as they did not quit their places, we advanced, and embraced in succession all those in the front line, stroking down their dress also, and receiving from them in return this established ceremony of friendship. This seemed to produce great delight ... and being informed that we were Europeans (Kablunae) they answered that they were men Innuit. Their numbers amounted to thirty-one; the eldest, called Illicta, being sixty-five years of age, six others between forty and fifty, and twenty of them between forty and twenty; the number being made up by four boys. Two were lame, and with the old man, were drawn by the others on sledges: one of them having lost a leg, from a bear.'[12]

Ross found the Inuit were much better dressed than the qallunaat – with their 'immense superstructure' of furs making them appear bigger than they were. They all carried spears with shafts formed of small pieces of wood or bone joined expertly together. At first glance, their knives seemed rather inoffensive, but he quickly discovered that hanging at their backs each had a more effective knife pointed with iron and sometimes edged with metal. 'Having no foresight of these visiters [sic], we had of course no presents at hand for them, and we therefore sent a man back to the ship for thirty-one pieces of iron hoop, that there might be a gift for each individual. But, in the mean time [sic] they consented to accompany us on board.'[13]

Neeveeovak says, 'The Inuit went to the qallunaat's ship and to show companionship the qallunaat wanted to give presents.' Describing the same visit, Lena says, 'When the white people met the Inuit, they shook hands. The Inuit and the white people were happy and excited to meet each other and the Inuit were told to get onto the ship. The white people noticed that all their weapons were made of bones and began giving them white people's weapons shaped like ulus [the woman's knife] with handles [perhaps adzes]. The people in this area had never had pieces of steel so large. But a certain man said, "I'm not a woman. I want a saw." He didn't have the proper tools to cut up what he was given to make a snow knife, so he wanted something long and flat. He didn't want that ulu, so he received nothing. He was too proud to be a man and didn't get anything!'

But, according to the oral tradition, there was that day an element ready for conflict. Jose Angutingunirk says, 'When the white men started giving out items, some Inuit wanted to confront the white people – they wanted to steal all the things from the ship. The white people then were ready to fight back because of the confrontation. That's the story I heard. One of the Inuit wanted to kill one of the white people, but he was afraid to do it – because these white people had guns. He was too afraid and never did it.'

Cordial Relations

But, on the whole, relations started well and continued warm. The next day, the *Victory* crew made an expedition to the homes of their visitors in the nearby, newly built snow village which Ross called North Hendon, after a recently developed London suburb. The Inuit had come only a few days before from other hunting grounds.

'The village soon appeared, consisting of twelve snow huts, erected at the bottom of a little bight on the shore, about two miles and a half from the ship. They had the appearance of inverted basins, and were placed without any order; each of them having a long crooked appendage, in which was the passage, at the entrance of which were the women, with the female children and infants. We were soon invited to visit these, for whom we had prepared presents of glass beads and needles.'[14] Ross created a sketch on the spot. He detected some uneasiness, but this disappeared as soon as he explained what he was doing. All 'were delighted with the identity of the representation when the sketch was finished; each recognising his own house.'

The qallunaat were eager to be welcoming hosts. They hoped for the help of the Inuit in provisioning and with the geography of the country. The man who had lost his leg to a bear – his name was Tulliahiu – was drawn over to the ship on a sledge. 'On examining the stump, the surgeon found it a sound one, long healed, while, the knee being bent, there would be no difficulty in applying a wooden leg. The carpenter was therefore sent for to measure him.' Two fittings later and the wooden leg was ready and inscribed with the word 'Victory.' 'The disabled person soon began to strut about the cabin, in apparent ecstasy ... All the surgery of this case lay with the carpenter ... but I doubt if any effort of surgery ever gave more satisfaction,' wrote Ross. Its owner became again an active hunter. 'I am sure the simple contrivance of this wooden leg, raised us higher in the estimation of this people, than all the wonders we had shown them.'[15]

Another perspective on Inuit-qallunaat relationships comes from the Rev. Ikey Nathaoraitok, who spent his youth in the Taloyoak area but is now the pastor at the Anglican Church of the Messiah in Gjoa Haven.

North Hendon. Snow Cottages of the Boothians. John Ross created a sketch of this Inuit camp of snow houses on the spot in January 1830. In his book, he called it after a new London suburb. Inuit 'were delighted with the identity of the representation when the sketch was finished; each recognising his own house.' Coloured lithograph after a sketch by John Ross.

He heard his stories from his father, whose ancestors met these first white men. The first visitors, he noted with his wife, Elizabeth, interpreting for us, were 'only men – they went to see the people on the ship and the qallunaat gave them stuff to take back to the camp. The people from the ship gave foodstuffs – groceries; but the Inuit wouldn't eat them because they had never tasted such food before. They collected it on the ground and it kept piling up. They had never smelled white man's food, and it had a strong odour so they left it where it was. The people on the ship asked why they wouldn't eat it? Then the qallunaat started getting caribou meat themselves and giving some to the Inuit. Even though it was caribou, the Inuit wouldn't eat it because it had the white man's smell.

'But slowly the Inuit began to eat the caribou meat, even though it smelled like white man ... Then the Inuit moved from their camp to where the ship was and they were friendly towards each other.'

Were there children born from these friendships? Elizabeth Nathaoraitok asks her husband and says, 'He doesn't know. But he and his cousin look kind of white. His cousin has light brown eyes and kind of a white skin – very unusual in an Inuk. So this might be from those qallunaat.'

With the first ship's visits, a lively trade began. The Inuit began to come daily with country food, fur clothing, and examples of their tools and equipment; the qallunaat paid in metal, knives, needles, and barrel hoops. The Inuit expressed continuous astonishment at the white man's possessions and the fittings of the ship. 'It is not politic to exhibit all our wonders at the beginning of our acquaintance,' Ross observes on 22 January. The following day he writes: 'The effects of the magnet were the chief novelty shown this day. The exhibition of snapdragon, as it is called, produced also great surprise; especially in the conjuror, who rewarded us with one of his conjuring songs.' And Ross decided now was the time to demonstrate the use of the pistol – 'since it was, sooner or later, necessary for them to know that our arms were superior to their own.'[16]

Perhaps it's at this point that the incident occurs which Jose Angutingunirk tells about: 'The next thing that happened, one of the white people started to show Inuit how a gun could hit hard at close range. That would teach them not to fight! The white person shot a rock and it splattered about the place. When they saw the rock shatter, the Inuit ran away. That's how I heard the story.'

Ross thought pilfering could become a problem and he took precautions: 'All the portable articles which were outside the ship, having been placed on the ice for convenience, were brought on board; while some men were appointed to watch ... We had no right to expect absolute honesty ... and, at any rate, were bound to expose them to temptations. ' On 12 February he recounts, 'We bought some articles brought by the natives, but did not suffer them to come on board. But this was not the only purpose of their visit; since there was a general restoration, as we understood, of all the other things which they had purloined; among which, a table knife from the mate's mess had alone been missed. With this there was a piece of iron, another of an iron hoop, and a sheave of a block. The cause of this repentance and restoration was, we found, to be attributed to the guns which had been fired for the purpose of the experiments on sound. One of them having attended Commander Ross to the observatory, and having asked what the "guns said," was informed that they were naming the thieves who had taken our property, of whatever nature, from the ship; on which there was a general convocation held at the village, and it was agreed to return every [sic] thing. We had to regret that we possessed no such powers of conjuration over the much less pardonable thieves of our own dear native land.'[17]

The white men's inexperience on the land sometimes made them easy marks. Ross notes that the crew showed Inuit how to fish with nets, a technique unknown to them, which initially left them unimpressed. Father Papion, OMI, who came to the Arctic as a young missionary, and lived for some years at the mission the Oblates operated at Thom Bay, tells the story an elderly Inuk called Itinnaq passed on of how, in spring, qallunaat from the ship arrived at a river where Inuit using the kakivak were spearfishing. 'The sailors were putting their nets into the river. The Inuit were laughing at them: "How to get fish with knotted strings?" As a matter of fact, they got nothing ... So those sailors decided to buy some fish from the Inuit. In the middle of August – full moon, big tides – the Inuit would go to the river to build a stone-trap to get the Arctic char going up to the lakes. Some years they'd get so many fish that they'd have some caches left over, or some caches got too much snow and were discovered only in summertime. And that is what happened that time; the Inuit sold to the sailors year-old rotten fish. The sailors were surprised that those fish were frozen, but anyway they took them and went away pulling their sledge with a heavy load. It was a good bargain for the Inuit ... The sailors got some sleep before

Early white men, the crew of the *Victory* among them, demonstrated the use of nets for catching fish. Inuit frequently preferred to use the nets for catching birds. *The First Explorers*. Stencil by Sowdjuk Nakashuk; printed by Jacoposie Tiglik, Pangnirtung, 1983.

they got home. In the morning, they were surprised those fish got rotten so quickly.'[18]

But by the end of February, in the midst of their first winter, the qallunaat were grateful for good neighbours. During the month, the Inuit had brought them 'two white bears, three gluttons, a dozen of foxes, and fifty seals ... We have come to a perfect understanding respecting the price of each article of sale which they brought.' Pilfering, Ross hoped, had come to an end, 'but it was certain that they considered these acts no vast crime, since the detection generally produced laughter.'[19] Anything more worrying than pilfering was rare, although on a sledging expedition James Clark Ross encountered one instance of threatening behaviour when he visited a camp where there had been a recent death. Some Inuit blamed the white man's magic.

Throughout the record he eventually published as *A Narrative of a Second Voyage in Search of a North-West Passage*, Ross pays tribute to the

Inuit for the help they provided: they brought the explorers food – seals and fish and fresh meat – guided them and helped them on sledging expeditions, made them maps, and helped them with the geography of the country. They were kind, he said, and the cause of kindness in others.[20]

When her children were small, Lena Kingmiatook camped in Lord Mayor Bay and knows the terrain well. She says, 'In that area there's a point and it's a very good seal hunting area in the wintertime, so they probably met each other quite often. And also in that area there's a small bay and near that, also very close to the bay, there's a lake with very good quality water and at the same time that lake has fish. These white people used it for getting their drinking water because the water is so clean.'

Ross had luckily come to harbour at a favourite Inuit camping area (Ross gave it the name Thom Bay after one of his officers). But how despairing Ross would have been had he known when he first met the Inuit that he was destined, because of ice conditions, to spend three winters in their hunting territory in three different harbours on a mere twenty miles of coast: the first winter at Felix Harbour slightly south of Thom Bay; the second winter at Sheriff's Harbour, slightly north (he was able to move only four miles through the ice); and finally at Victoria Harbour, where he had to abandon his ship.

In the first two years of this enforced captivity, the expedition extended knowledge of the area; importantly, in May 1830, James Clark Ross, on a marathon sledge journey, reached and named Cape Felix, the northwestern point of King William Island, and shortly after, Victory Point. Both sites would figure in the Franklin tragedy for this was the fatal shore where Franklin would come to grief; the ice floes in the winters could be carried half a mile inland. In May 1831, the younger Ross discovered the position of the north magnetic pole, a significant scientific achievement. But the expedition did not solve the vital questions: Was Boothia an isthmus? Or separated from the continental mainland by water? Similarly, was the land the Rosses called King William Land part of the mainland – or an island?

By 30 September 1831, located in Victoria Harbour, John Ross knew the expedition could not stay another winter in the area. Of his situation in the ice, he wrote, 'We might as well have been walled in with masonary on dry land.'[21] His great concern was the health of his men. Scurvy had broken out and spirits were low. He searched for 'topics of consolation,' repeating again and again all that was positive about their situation: 'We are really on our return ... there is no reason why that should not be completed in the following year. There was still before us the Fury's remaining store; and there were boats, to carry us into Davis's strait, should we be obliged to abandon the ship; where we should either meet a whaler, or reach the Danish settlements in Greenland.' The result was that 'the hopeful did not hope more, and the despondent continued to despair.'

As the Inuit had moved to new hunting grounds there were no more visits to relieve the tedium.

The Retreat

In January 1832 Ross began to organize the retreat. 'We prepared our mining tools for the purpose of making a place of concealment,' he wrote as the New Year arrived. The weather on 15 January was mild, 'and the work on the tunnel went on.' Boats were repaired, new ones made for carrying provisions, and sledges constructed for transporting them. 'The abandonment of the vessel had long ceased to be a matter of hesitation; and the object now was to proceed to Fury beach,' Ross declared on 22 April.

Ross and a party of officers and men began leaving depots over thirty miles of the route; it was arduous work, entailing back and forth journeys amounting to 329 miles. Later Ross said that was the worst part of the road.

Despite the lack of contact with the Inuit at that time, Lena Kingmiatook has apparently heard details about the preparations for departure. 'That spring the ice was kind of late and they were trying to go back or go on to where they were trying to go. All of a sudden the main part of the ice started breaking up and it all piled up against the ship. While it was crushing the ship, those white people picked up everything they seemed to treasure, whatever they could carry, and brought it to the shore over a smooth part as fast as they could. And in that area there was a bit of gravel, a bit of sand, and they dug down deep into the permafrost. When they reached permafrost, they'd wait until it thawed out and then they'd dig some more. Then they buried their treasure.'

In the last weeks of May, Ross noted that 'chronometers and astronomical instruments which could be spared and could not be taken, were concealed in the place that we had made, together with some gunpowder.'[22] Masts, sails, and rigging were placed in the *Krusenstern*. 'We had now secured everything on shore which could be of use to us in càse of our return, or which if we did not, would prove of use to the natives.'

On 29 May, Ross abandoned ship, leaving her 'fixed in immobile ice, till time should perform on her his usual handiwork.' The *Victory* crew set out over icy terrain where 'all was rock: it seemed as if there was never to be water again.'[23]

The Treasure Troves

The Ross expedition left the Inuit two principal treasure troves: one at Felix Harbour on McDiarmid's Island, where Ross turfed out his engine; and one at Victoria Harbour, where he abandoned ship. Gideon Qauqjuaq of Taloyoak describes these sites: 'In the area of Kablunaaqh-iuvik there are a lot of old pieces of engine still there on an island, but further from where Abiluktuq first saw the ship, further from that famous area, thirty or thirty-five miles further up north, there's an area where they supposedly buried some of their equipment. We were told there was once an arrow to mark the spot, but the arrow has disappeared long ago, maybe because some animals chewed it up or the polar bears took it away. So there is no marker; there are some old pieces of iron around, but a lot of this has vanished. The Inuit never found exactly where they buried their stuff, probably because they never looked in the summertime.'

Patterk Qagutaq, thought to be the oldest man in Pelly Bay, tells a story that suggests Inuit purposely gave Ross's cache a wide berth. 'When summer came, the ship was wrecked ... The white people started to take their relics off the ship. I've heard that they also buried items in boxes. Afterwards the Inuit started to seek for things and dig them up. But when they started digging, the boxes began exploding. The boxes were labelled – they had labels on them. So they stopped looking for the boxes because they started to explode.'

Today nobody knows the location of Ross's treasure, although, according to Alex Buchan, a retired Hudson's Bay Company trader who lives in Taloyoak, both Inuit and HBC men have searched.

Lena Kingmiatook says from stories she's heard she has a good idea of where the burial place of the valuable things might be. 'The reason she wants to find it,' interpreter Tommy Anguttitauruq explains, 'is because she's very interested in one certain thing – a big long telescope. Maybe they don't make that certain type of telescope today and to some people it could be quite valuable. Lena's late husband was raised by old people, and he was told what was in the treasure by his great-grandparents and grandparents and parents. Just before he was medevacked out to Yellowknife, he told her if she knows of white people going to look for the treasure, she should go along with them to help them. Then she'd be able to buy herself an ATV [all terrain vehicle] and a snowmobile.'

The Inuit observed the final fate of Ross's vessels. The little *Krusenstern* was pulled up on shore, but the *Victory* was abandoned beset in the ice.

Otto Apsatauk lives in Pelly Bay, but in traditional times he used to frequent Thom Bay, and the area he knew as Killanaaqtuuq – 'having desirable things.' 'My uncle Anaija and my father-in-law Kipingaipik were the two people who used to tell me the stories of Killanaaqtuuq. There had been a shipwreck there around Thom Bay, and the hunters could see the mast out in the area. In wintertime they'd go to it and try to break it off.

'For years hunters tried to take away the mast, hauling and pulling at it. The mast was not metal – it was a wooden mast – and they wanted it so they could use it for sleds or harpoons, any kind of gear. They kept trying to bend it and it would get so flexible but it wouldn't break off. Every time when the summer came, the mast would get shorter and shorter; I guess the mast was sinking, sinking. Each winter the hunters went back to it and the mast was shorter and shorter but they kept trying to break it off. The last time, after summer was over, they went back to it to try once again, but the mast was gone. The hunters think it broke off because of the icebergs.

'There were also metal pieces that were left on the land [at Felix Harbour], but I haven't heard if the Inuit took any. What they really wanted was metal, but they couldn't strip pieces from the steel in the Thom Bay area.'

With his knowledge of the area and local people, Father Papion, now retired, admits he might have more stories of the Ross expedition than he does, except 'I never took any notes because at that time, like the Inuit, the main thing was to survive – myself and my dogs – so that means fishing, hunting, were more important than stories.

'When I arrived at Thom Bay, I was surprised that some Inuit were using kudluks – the stone lamps – made of thick red copper. The Inuit told that their ancestors got that copper from the bow of the *Victory*, deserted by its equipage ... This ship – not anchored – over the years went away with the ice and sank close to the southern part of a small island. Passing by dog team between the mainland and that island, my companion pointing to the spot, told me, "It is there that the ship sank," and he said, "I heard from old people that for some years the end of the mast was pointing out of the ice."'

Father Papion recalls metal engine parts lying around at Felix Harbour and says that he once saw 'shining tracks of metal on the side of a big boulder.' His Inuk companion explained that a long time ago, without files, Inuit had managed to shape some steel pieces by rubbing them on the rock. 'What patience!'

The *Victory* and what was left behind at what one interpreter called the two 'land stores' helped out generations of Inuit – and also the occasional qallunaat. Father Papion says he found 'some useful pieces of steel: an anchor as pillar for my ice-house; two big hooks [ice anchors used to anchor the ship on pack ice]; I used them to anchor the dog chain.' (Some years after he had retrieved them, the commissioner of the Northwest Territories of the time asked him if 'it was OK with me to take those two "hooks" to Yellowknife; of course, they were not my property!')

When Father Papion first arrived in the Canadian Arctic, he had been expecting to be sent to another country. 'I didn't know anything about the expeditions of Franklin and other explorers.' But his knowledge increased after a visitor arrived one summer to collect northern plants and flowers. 'I was doing the same thing but for medicinal reasons.' He gave the collector one of his specimens and sometime later received as a present Ross's *Second Voyage in Search of a North-West Passage*. 'I read from Captain Ross's journal that the carpenter of the ship made a wooden leg for an Inuk who had only one leg. That Inuk died not far from Spence Bay [now Taloyoak]. The name of the ship *Victory* was carved on that wooden leg: I asked an Inuk if he knew something about that wooden leg. "Yes," he said, "it is on the stones of a grave not far from Spence Bay. I can go and get it for you." I agreed, but on his way back he sold it to the Hudson Bay manager. Where is that wooden leg now? I don't know.'

Peter Nichols, the retired former manager of the Arctic Division of the Hudson's Bay Company, answers that question: 'John Stanners was one of the first managers after we opened Spence Bay. This wooden leg – this peg leg – was brought in to him and on my next visit there he gave it to me, suggesting, "Give it to the Museum." I did.'[24]

The word 'Victory' proclaims its origin. Nichols says, 'It was made by the ship's carpenter. Originally it had a muskox skull at the base. By the time we got it, that wasn't with it. You see, if it were just a straight stick, it would have gone through the snow. The skull was put on the bottom of the peg leg so it would hold up on the snow.'

Throughout his journal, Ross notes occasions when the leg is repaired, refitted, bound with copper. And on 13 August 1831, before what was to be the expedition's last winter in the area, he wrote, 'In this visit to the tents, we found that the wooden leg was once more ailing, in some manner of which I did not particularly inquire, since the carpenter-doctor was at hand to examine into the grievance, and was ready to repair it as best he knew how.'[25]

The carpenter-doctor, whose name was Chimham Thomas, died of scurvy and other physical distress at Fury Beach during the expedition's last winter, but his masterwork still gets careful attention in the collections of the Manitoba Museum of Man and Nature.

End of the Journey

Lena Kingmiatook tells me that Inuit have never really known what happened to the white men after they left Victoria Harbour. 'The white men lived mostly by themselves – the same as the Inuit lived. We're not too sure what happened to them. They probably starved or froze to death.'

But such was not the case. After Ross abandoned ship, he marched his men a distance of 180 miles (not counting much backtracking to bring forward supplies) to Fury Beach, where in 1825 Parry had left the *Fury*. Here Ross knew stores were still abundant; he had checked on them and augmented his supplies on his passage into Prince Regent's Inlet. Ross's crew built a wooden shelter there, where they had to pass a fourth winter, and then, the following summer, they rowed and sailed after the whalers in Lancaster Sound.

With the coming of the missionaries and traders, some Inuit heard the rudiments of the end of the journey. Patterk Qagutaq relates: 'A ship met a lifeboat with people in it. When the lifeboat got to the ship, the Captain said, "These people are not our people." They were so dirty; their beards were grown and their moustaches were grown. The ship was going to leave them behind.

'Just in time a man from the lifeboat showed the Captain some papers. When the Captain read the papers, he understood right away. These

The *Victory*'s crews rescued by the *Isabella*. Lithograph from a sketch by John Ross.

were their people. He boarded them and from then on they started taking care of them and cleaning them up. That's Father Henri's story [Father Pierre Henry, OMI].'

In his *Narrative of a Second Voyage in Search of a North-West Passage*, which he published in 1835, a little more than a year after his return, Ross gives a thrilling and moving account of the moment of rescue at the end of the expedition's long ordeal.

At eleven o'clock on 26 August 1833, after the crew in three boats had rowed since six in the morning after vessels that failed to sight them, Ross says, 'We saw her [a ship] heave to with all sails aback, and lower down a boat, which rowed immediately towards our own.

'She was soon alongside, when the mate in command addressed us, by presuming we had met with some misfortune and lost our ship. This being answered in the affirmative, I requested to know the name of his vessel, and expressed our wish to be taken on board. I was answered that it was "the Isabella of Hull, once commanded by Captain Ross"; on which I stated I was the identical man in question, and my people the crew of the Victory. That the mate, who commanded this boat, was as much astonished at this information as he appeared to be, I do not doubt ... he assured me that I had been dead for two years. I easily convinced him, however, that what ought to have been true, according to his estimate, was a somewhat premature conclusion.'

The crew of the *Victory* boarded the *Isabella* to rousing cheers. 'Unshaven since I know not when, dirty, dressed in the rags of wild beasts instead of the tatters of civilization, and starved to the very bones, our gaunt and grim looks, when contrasted with those of the well-dressed and well-fed men around us, made us all feel, I believe for the first time, what we really were.' Then, in short order, 'all was done, for all of us, which care and kindness could perform.'

Opinionated John Ross never achieved a total 'fit' with his brother naval officers, but few begrudged him his knighthood and the warmth of his reception back home in England. 'From the very borders of a not distant grave,' he had brought his men back to 'life and friends and civilization.'[26]

While telling me the story of the expedition's fate as he had learned it from the missionaries, Patterk passed on other facts he considered pertinent. 'Before the qallunaat got into the lifeboat, while they were walking up north, they ran out of their own food, and had to eat country food. Some of them were vegetarians and couldn't eat country food and they died. These were the people from Thom Bay; they were heading back up, but some of them died from starvation.'

This account surprised me. Although Ross lost two men from illness while the *Victory* was locked in the ice and the carpenter Chimham Thomas died at Fury Beach, none died on the trek. Was this simply a case of inexactitude creeping into oral history over the years? Or was it blended oral history? Were there British explorers who starved to death on the Boothia Peninsula? Some students of the Franklin disaster believe that there may have been.

George Back's Rescue Mission – and Its Legacy

Indirectly, one more treasure trove resulted from the Ross expedition. This lies a considerable distance south from the various *Victory* anchorages, on what at the time was called the Great Fish River.

Rick Dwyer, a former Hudson's Bay Company man who makes his home in Gjoa Haven, recalls he was downright skeptical when his wife, Martha Tululik, who died a few years ago, mentioned that when her family went to the place where they camped when the char was running she used to dig for beads. '"You don't dig for beads, they're manufactured," I told her. She said, "We always found beads." Her grandfather said the same thing: "When I was a little boy, we used to dig for beads." I thought they must mean coloured pebbles.'[27]

Those beads were trade beads, one of the most prized gifts of the explorers, left by George Back on his expedition to rescue Ross and his men. In 1832, as John Ross accepted the inevitability of the abandonment of his vessel, concern began to grow in England. A committee promoting an expedition by land made plans for a rescue operation, and Commander George Back volunteered to lead it. As a midshipman, Back had been with Franklin on his overland expeditions of 1819 and 1824. He had heard the rumours that Ross and his men had perished but believed that Ross, if he could, would head up the coast for the stores of the *Fury* and might still be alive. Accordingly, his instructions were to travel overland to reach the *Fury*, exploring as he went the Great Fish River should it prove a useful route to the polar sea. He left Liverpool on 17 February 1833 with eighteen men and, as his second-in-command, twenty-three-year-old Dr Richard King, recently qualified as a surgeon-naturalist. (During the Franklin searches, King was to prove a particularly irritating thorn-in-the-flesh for the Admiralty.) The expedition was financed by private subscription and a grant from the Treasury, and was

George Back at the mouth of the Back River; engraving from a sketch by George Back.

provisioned and taken under the protection of the Hudson's Bay Company. In April 1834, Back was en route but still quartered for winter in his newly built Fort Reliance when the news reached him that Ross and his expedition had miraculously arrived back in England. His orders now were to continue on in hopes of mapping more Arctic coastline. He reached the mouth of the river now called after him and discovered Chantrey Inlet.

On his way down river, Inuit had received Back well, but on his return, he found them reluctant to renew the aquaintance: 'We reached the lower fall, where in our descent we had found the Eskimaux. They had disappeared, which I much regretted, not only because my pockets were laden with presents for them, but because I wanted to make some more sketches. Having proceeded four miles farther to a line of heavy rapids, an Eskimaux was seen on the hills; and shortly after the two tents which we had before visited were discovered pitched on the eastern bank of a strong rapid, the eddies of which probably furnished an ample supply of fish. It was impossible for us to cross without endangering the boat, and we commenced making two long portages, while the natives watched us with much composure from the opposite heights, where they were all seated in a line. As we could not attract them to us by any signs, a number of iron hoops were placed on a pile of stones, with various coloured ribbonds [sic] attached to them; besides twenty-three awls, fifteen fishhooks, three dozen brass rings, and two pounds of beads. All this was done under their eyes; they could scarcely fail therefore to understand its friendly import, and that our intentions were to benefit them.'[28]

But a second, more disturbing description of the encounter by the rapids comes from Back's second-in-command, Dr Richard King:[29] 'The Esquimaux were perceived flying in the utmost consternation to the far-distant hills, where they could just be made out without telescopes as living objects. Their tents were deserted and their canoes secreted, conduct so different from that of our first interview that we were convinced something extraordinary must have taken place.'

No clue to what had happened surfaced until the expedition was back in England. Then it was discovered that three men sent off independently on an assignment '... fell in, during their march with a party of Esquimaux and for an instant retreated. The natives, in following them, fired a few arrows, upon which the men turned and discharged their guns, killed three of the party, and wounded others ... The natives thoroughly dismayed at seeing their countrymen fall around them, fled in the greatest disorder, and the men equally alarmed betook themselves to flight also.'

King gives the natives the benefit of the doubt: 'A practice exists with the Esquimaux to fire blunt arrows in token of their peaceful intentions; which in all probability was the case in this instance ...' But he notes: 'The Esqimaux had they been inclined, might have murdered us in our beds with the greatest ease for we were so little apprehensive of danger.'

Unaware of what had led to the cooling of relations, on leaving the rapids, King writes, 'a number of iron hoops were placed on a pile of stones, together with ribands of various colours, awls, fish-hooks, brass rings and beads, which, of course, would be construed into treachery on our part, for the purpose of alluring them across the river that they might fall an easier prey. During the whole of the 23rd August the Esquimaux were distinctly seen, by the aid of our telescopes, watching our motions and hiding their kieyacks (canoes) [sic] the sign of war.'

Just about a hundred years later, Knud Rasmussen heard an Inuit story of the Back expedition's return journey: 'They came up the river and they were in a great hurry, and the people were afraid of them for it had been heard tell that one had to be cautious of white men who retraced their steps: they were dangerous and easily angered. In those times there were wise shamans among the folks, and one of the eldest spoke a magic verse that was intended to charm the white men away, far away ...'[30]

Back River people live now chiefly in Baker Lake, but memories of life on the land are always to the fore, particularly among the community's older residents. 'The best time of all was living in Chantrey Inlet and playing on the rock cliffs,' the great artist Jessie Oonark told an interviewer. 'There's no place like Chantrey Inlet. There's all kinds of fish there – although the water is much lower than it was years ago ... There were so many fish that even the fish themselves would climb on top of the rocks and sort of dry out.' There was once 'a real powerful shaman' living near Baker Lake who was asked to check on people and conditions at Chantrey Inlet. 'He was asked to perform and he went up to see the Chantrey Inlet area in his performance. He flew up and came back; same night.' Oonark's eldest daughter, Janet Kigusiuq, an artist also, is known for much-admired images of the Back River. 'I grew up on the Back River in fish camp,' she said, explaining her choice of subject matter.[31]

So bountiful at the time of the fish run, the great river often turned

This scene takes place on the pebble beach where the artist's family fished each year. 'Here is Quinangnaq, my father's brother, holding the kakivak (fishing spear) and Josiah Nuillalik, my brother.' *Fishing for Arctic Char*, by Janet Kigusiuq, Baker Lake, 2000. Pencil crayon.

cruel; the starvations and death that occurred there, and elsewhere, in the year 1958 effectively led to the end of life on the land all over the North. With government assistance, Inuit moved into settlements. Oonark's half-brother, the artist Simon Tookoome, who once lived on the river's lakes, told me, 'We were affected but we survived ... Through prayer we got by; only by prayer. We'd catch caribou or fish. God gave us the food. We would run out of food but only for a short time. Fish would come, caribou would come. We were around Garry Lake but we never stopped; we went from place to place. The time I was most afraid was when my father said he didn't want to walk further distances just to starve to death. He wanted to camp and not move again, even if we starved. But we didn't do that ... we survived.'[32]

Memories like these, and even sadder ones, are the stuff of oral history in Baker Lake today. But echoes or snatches of old stories about the explorers – the first white men – descending the river still survive. (After the Back expedition, just over twenty years later, the James

Anderson expedition, in two canoes, travelled the river to verify stories of the Franklin disaster.) Silas Kulluk is not sure if he's ninety-one or ninety-nine, but with his granddaughter Nancy Tookoome interpreting, he says, 'I heard about early white men who came in canoes along the Back River. One of them visited an Inuit tent and gave a woman a paper. After he left, the woman threw the paper in the fire. Later she began to think, "Maybe that paper was needles."' Others recall that 'some of those white people spat a lot, making the ground muddy – maybe the beginning of roads?' And Back's expedition left a specific legacy: up to today, people dig up beads.

Rick Dwyer's wife spent her childhood in the Back River area. 'The place they used to go to was a very large waterfall – actually more like a rapid on the scale of Niagara Falls with the water shooting forward and the spray going up twenty or thirty feet,' says Rick Dwyer. 'Using their fish spears, they could get two hundred big char a day without trying. There are so many fish ... there's an area where they go over red rock; all of a sudden you see the rocks turning black with fish. Then in about ten minutes they get red again. Unless you've seen it, you can't believe it.

'When I finally went to this camp on the Back River – we flew down – my wife said, "Let's dig for beads." I said OK. You got a flat piece of wood and you gently scraped the sand away. About eight or twelve inches down, you began seeing beads. I looked at them and I said, "My God! They're beads!" How did they get there?

'At this place where the people camp, if there's a very large run-off, which is almost every year, when the overflow is in full spate, the area is an island and a lot of gravel is washed right over; then it stops running and the place is a peninsula again. This is where the people were camping back in George Back's time.

'Some very clever arts and crafts people came north, and a ceramics lady looked at the beads with a magnifying glass. She was able to tell what they were right away: they were made in Venice around 1800.'

3 The Franklin Era: Burial of a Great White Shaman

'The way my father told it they buried their leader, the captain, on a hill – on the rocks – somewhere on the northwest of King William Island. They gave him a proper burial. They buried him with respect. There was a proper burial northside of King William Island. Or somewhere else. Nobody knows exactly where. A lot of people went looking for him but nobody ever found him. In the same place, they packed up his logbook or some papers. They wrapped them up properly so they wouldn't get wet or damaged by the weather, so that people who found him would be able to understand exactly what had happened. They probably didn't leave them on the ground so probably they covered them with rocks.

'We heard they buried the captain on a hill – a long narrow hill. So if people were looking in the right place, they would probably find him. If he was a captain, if he was buried properly, there should be signs of something – the ground stirred round, rocks as a marker. We heard they buried the captain carefully. That's the way we heard it. We heard he was buried on a long narrow hill. The people who went looking for him probably were not looking in the right places.'

Jimmy Qirqut of Gjoa Haven on King William Island is passing on a story he heard as a child from his father which he believes describes the burial of Sir John Franklin, commander of the last expedition which the Royal Navy, in 1845, sent specifically in search of the Northwest Passage. Only fourteen years after the expedition departed would information reach a British public, clamorous for news, that Sir John had died 11 June 1847, and that ten months later his crews abandoned their vessels *Erebus* and *Terror* amid unyielding ice.

'The Search for Franklin: H.M.S. *Assistance* in Tow of *Pioneer* Passing John Barrow Mount.' Painted on glass by an unkown artist and designed to be projected
as a lantern slide. The *Assistance* and the *Pioneer* belonged to Captain Horatio
Austin's squadron and numbered among some thirteen ships that in 1850
entered Lancaster Sound searching for Franklin. Manufactured by Smith and
Beck, London, makers of telescopes. The great public concern for the fate of
Franklin and his men kept the tragedy to the fore in the English-speaking world
well into the twentieth century.

I ask Jimmy who were the witnesses to this story, and he says, 'We do
not know. It happened years and years ago. The people who heard the
story passed it on to the next people and these people to the next people. The people who told the stories never mentioned meeting the crew,
or trading with them or anything at all. Nobody saw the ship – what
happened to it; or how they died or how they starved. Other people
tell the same stories. But everyone who heard the stories heard them
passed on from someone else. They don't know who. Not many people
have long stories – only short stories. Little stories, here and there. We
don't know much at all.'

Like so much associated with Sir John Franklin's last expedition, the
story raises questions.[1] Is it originally a King William Island tradition,

or did it make its way up from the coast of Hudson Bay to eventually become one? Give or take a rumour or two, Jimmy Qirqut's story has similarities to a story circulated among the Inuit whalers in Roes Welcome Sound which partly inspired the 1878 Schwatka expedition in search of the Franklin records.

Though many have looked, Sir John's grave is still to be found, and some investigators believe Franklin was buried at sea.

Certainly on King William Island the tradition exists that Franklin was buried ashore. 'They buried their great white shaman on the island, though which island we do not know,' says Tommy Anguttitauruq. This was the information his grandmother passed on, and his caveat allows for an Inuit rumour said to have been picked up in 1949 by Inspector H.A. Larsen of the Royal Canadian Mounted Police when he examined Cape Felix, the most northern tip of King William Island, that Franklin was buried on one of the two islets, not much more than reefs, which lie about two miles north of the Cape. Cape Felix was the nearest point of land to Franklin's two icebound ships and there was evidence here of a working camp. Tommy says only that the Inuit word for King William Island is simply Qikiqtaq – 'island' – and there are many islands around King William Island. Gjoa Haven's Louis Kamookak, who is the community's resident researcher on Franklin mysteries, and who has conducted his own searches for Franklin's grave, says the uninvestigated islets off Cape Felix are difficult of access because of ice and weather. Larsen found them so; he thought he could discern them about two miles north of the Cape, but the state of the ice prevented him going there.[2]

Jimmy continues with a story from the more recent past that used to be told by a well-remembered Ghoa Haven elder. It is suggestive of an honour guard, perhaps, and burial of an officer or officers. 'An old lady – her name was Joanne Humuuk – told a story that she and her husband [stories told by Louis Kamookak, her great-grandson, suggest she might have been with her father] were one time at the north side of King William Island looking for driftwood to make a kayak. They used to do that and it was in the spring when the snow was off the ground. They found a sandy beach and on the sandy beach they found a lot of pellets – musket pellets – along the shore on the sandy beach. At the time they knew these were coming from the people who lost their ship on the north side of King William Island.'

We don't know exactly where Joanne Humuuk found the musket

pellets, but if in the vicinity of Cape Felix, it has to be noted that the first searchers found 'numerous traces of a shooting or magnetic station near Cape Felix.' However, since Larsen's visit, investigators have agreed that Franklin (and also others who died before abandonment of the iced-in ships) may have been buried on land. At Cape Felix Larsen found, according to a report in the *Geographical Journal*, 'the remains of a human skull embedded in moss between some rocks about half a mile from the sea ... Larsen's discovery is of great interest, for none of the previous searchers [at Cape Felix] has found the bones of members of the Franklin expedition ... For this reason it has hitherto been generally believed that Franklin himself [and other officers and men who died before the ships were abandoned] ... were buried at sea. This discovery shows, however, and Larsen believes, that some may have been buried on land although, as he states, the finding of bones or graves would be only accidental, for the terrain is difficult to examine and any crosses or memorials would long ago have been removed by Eskimos.'[3]

Jimmy heard the Franklin stories he tells from his father when his family had their principal camp near the Kaleet River, which drains into the Sherman Basin. 'My father told the stories when we were children in the igloos and tents to entertain us and also so we would know something of the past,' he says. 'After I was married and we lived in houses in Gjoa Haven, he told my children that searchers had come to look for lost crews but never found them. He wanted someone to remember them.'

The Lost Expedition

On 19 May 1845 the *Erebus* and the *Terror*, with Sir John Franklin as expedition commander and Captain F.M. Crozier as second-in-command, left England amid optimism and high hope. The journals of Parry and Ross had excited the public imagination, and the public at large and many in naval circles confidently believed this was the expedition that would complete the passage. After the last twenty-five years of exploration there was not, some thought, that much territory still unknown to be traversed. The expedition was the best equipped, the best supplied, of any to venture into polar regions. (The vessels had rather cumbersome auxiliary steam engines that had formerly powered locomotives.) Biographies of the vessels' officers show all were highly qualified, and second-in-command Captain Francis Crozier, captain of the *Terror*, was a veteran Arctic and Antarctic explorer; he had been with

Parry at Igloolik; with Parry on his 1824–5 attempt to make the Passage when he had had to abandon the *Fury* and her supplies at Fury Beach; and he had been with James Clark Ross on his successful Antarctic expedition. A significant number of officers and men had previous Arctic experience, including the ice master on the *Terror*, Thomas Blanky, who had been with John Ross during his famous four-winter ordeal. Before setting sail, Sir John and his officers had daguerreotypes taken (to be found today in the archives of the National Maritime Museum, Greenwich), and on hand on shipboard for documentation purposes was photographic equipment. What stories photographs might have told if, as with the expedition's records, any had ever reached the outside world.

Amid the general euphoria, Sir John Ross, knighted after his miraculous return from four winters in the ice, was a realist: he counselled leaving notes in cairns en route and depots in case of necessary retreat; and promised to go in search of his old colleague if the need arose. (His advice was ignored – he would continue to irritate his contemporaries until the day he died – but he proved as good as his word: he was the first to raise the alarm, and he sailed on the Franklin searches in his seventies.) And in the public arena there was one highly audible naysayer: Dr Richard King, who had explored the Great Fish River – now renamed the Back River – with Sir George Back in 1834 on what had been initially a search for John Ross. King argued strongly for land expeditions, and his arguments – rudely expressed – gave offence. He invited the fellows of the Royal Geographical Society to reflect on the fact that most sea expeditions had been 'unsuccessful or attended with prodigious loss or risk – how great an expense they unavoidably incur compared with the amount of real advantage.'[4]

King had a point. Since Parry's great triumph in 1819–20, when he reached Melville Island (in 1845 still the farthest west), expeditions by ship had not furthered the search for the Passage by much. Many expeditions had been near disasters: Ross and also Parry on his last 1824–5 attempt on the Passage had lost their ships (Parry had left the *Fury* at Fury Beach, which saved the lives of Ross and his crew); both Lyon in 1824 and Back in 1836–7 had led expeditions that came to grief.

At the outset of the Admiralty's nineteenth-century quest for the Passage, it had, in fact, sponsored two overland expeditions under the leadership of the young John Franklin, and while the first journey had been a particularly horrific trek with a death toll of ten, the second, well-executed expedition in 1825–7 had mapped over a thousand miles of the Arctic coastline, an outstanding achievement. Then, in 1836, as further support of King's contention, the Hudson's Bay Company had sent Thomas Simpson and Peter Dease on expeditions of negligible cost compared to the naval ventures. In 1837 and 1838 they travelled the Arctic coastline, discovering astounding amounts of new coast. However, at the end of their ventures, the two stubborn questions remained: Was King William an island? Was Boothia an isthmus? In addition, there was little knowledge of the Arctic archipelago farther north and west. Was there open ocean? Were there islands? Old Arctic hands held strong and contradictory opinions. But in 1839 the Admiralty's interest for the moment was in a new direction: it dispatched James Clark Ross on a successful discovery expedition to the Antarctic. It was only after his return in 1843 that a new Northwest Passage search was planned. The Admiralty was in the business of naval expeditions, and so, as the Admiralty favoured, it was by sea.

The command was given to Sir John Franklin, but there had been reservations. The Admiralty's first choice was James Clark Ross, but just returned from Antarctica, and newly married, he declared himself unavailable. Franklin was fifty-nine; Parry in 1819–20, when he sailed through Lancaster Sound to winter at Melville Island, had been twenty-eight. The men who pioneered the search for the Passage were growing old.

The Disaster

Erebus and *Terror* and their crews entered Lancaster Sound in late July of 1845 and disappeared.[5] In 1847 the Admiralty began to organize a program of searches which got under way in 1848 and would number in the vicinity of forty by the time they ended. The British public waited for news from the searches with intense concern, as did many in the United States, where there was widespread sympathy. In *Sir John Franklin's Last Arctic Expedition*, a masterly assessment of all related published and unpublished documents and sources, which appeared in 1939 and would influence all future studies of the tragedy, R.J. Cyriax wrote, 'It is difficult to realize at the present day, more than ninety years after Sir John Franklin sailed on his last voyage, what a painful sensation was caused by his disappearance. His rescue became a national question of the first importance, and carried the good wishes of all civilized peoples.'[6] (It was discovered, fairly quickly, in 1850, that Franklin had spent the first winter at Beechey Island: after this, the expedition vanished.)[7] The only official record ever found would be discovered after Britain had officially declared the searches ended. However, in 1854, after six years of searches – the costs had been enormous, vessels had been abandoned, crews had endured icy agony and impairment to health – the Admiralty received information that left little doubt of the expedition's fate.

In 1848, the Hudson's Bay Company (HBC) trader and explorer Dr John Rae had participated in one of the first searches for the lost expedition, travelling along the North American continental coast by small boat. But it was only in the spring of 1854, while exploring for the HBC, that he heard the first accounts of the expedition's disastrous end. These came from an Inuk called Innookpoozheejook, whom he met in the Pelly Bay area, and later from Inuit who visited him at his base camp at Repulse Bay. Rae traded for a large collection of relics (Franklin's Badge of Knight Commander of the Royal Hanoverian Guelphic Order, crested silver forks and spoons, and other shiny items) and returned to London to report his findings. During his exploratory journey, Rae had found the answers to two vital questions that had eluded earlier explorers and bedevilled the search for the Northwest Passage. Boothia was an isthmus. King William was an island. Had his geographic information been available earlier, there would not have been a Franklin tragedy. There was little interest, however, in these discoveries; they were completely overshadowed by the information contained in his letter to the Admiralty, datelined Repulse Bay:

'In the spring, four winters past (spring 1850) a party of "white men," amounting to about forty, were seen travelling southward over the ice, and dragging a boat with them, by some Esquimaux who were killing seals near the north shore of King William's Land (which is a large island). None of the party could speak the Esquimaux language intelligibly, but by signs the natives were made to understand that their ship, or ships, had been crushed by ice, and that they were now going to where they expected to find deer to shoot. From the appearance of the men, all of whom, except one officer, looked thin, they were then supposed to be getting short of provisions, and purchased a small seal from the natives. At a later date the same season, but previous to the breaking up of the ice, the bodies of some thirty persons were discovered on the continent, and five on an island near it, about a long day's journey to the N.W. of a large stream, which can be no other than Back's Great Fish River ... Some of the bodies had been buried (probably those of the first victims of famine), some were in a tent, or tents, others under the boat, which had been turned over to form a shelter, and several lay scattered about in different directions. Of those found on the island one was supposed to have been an officer, as he had a telescope strapped over his shoulders, and his double-barrelled gun lay underneath him.

'From the mutilated state of many of the corpses, and the contents of the kettles, it is evident that our wretched countrymen had been driven to the last resource – cannibalism – as a means of prolonging existence.'[8]

The Admiralty released his letter in the *Times* the day after receiving it, and immediately Rae became the victim of a shoot-the-messenger syndrome. (Almost alone among the major figures of Arctic exploration, he did not receive a knighthood.) His revelations of cannibalism among men of the Royal Navy were deeply shocking to the British public. To compound the Admiralty's problems, King, who considered the Admiralty 'manifestly the most inefficient of the Government boards,'[9] had urgently and frequently called for a relief expedition up the Back River (offering himself as its leader), but his counsel was not taken up. It proved to be correct, and a multitude of letters to the British press pointed this out. 'Half the tragedy of the Franklin search,' wrote Ann Parry, great-great-granddaughter of Sir Edward, more than a century later in her book *Parry of the Arctic*, 'is that the wrong people were so often right and the right people wrong.'[10]

With Rae's revelations, the Admiralty prepared to let the search lapse. England was at war in the Crimea, all members of the Franklin expedition were considered dead, and, last but not at all least, costs had been huge: a number of search vessels had been abandoned, some lives lost, and the lives of many of the searchers saved seemingly only by miracles. When the Crimean war ended in 1856, there were naval officers who pressed for another search. But the Admiralty put an end to this promptly: there was now no possibility of saving life, and the risks would not be justified. But the Admiralty was immediately confronted by one of the most potent personalities of the searches: Jane Franklin, Sir John's widow.

Even today on King William Island, Jane Franklin's story moves those who hear it. Says Louis Kamookak, who in the summer of 2000 guided the Canadian RCMP vessel *St Roch II* to graves of expedition members on the Todd Islands, 'She sent out searches and I respect that: she deserves that he's buried beside her.'

Lady Franklin had spent much of her personal wealth equipping, with the help of friends, two previous search vessels. Now, with friends, she bought the *Fox* and organized her own expedition. She appointed as commander Francis Leopold McClintock, initially a protégé of Sir James Clark Ross, and a Franklin search veteran. McClintock was a willing recruit. 'Unless the search is completed I don't think the Arctic men will ever receive the credit they deserve, also ... I do not think any future Govt. will ever reopen the Arctic regions,' McClintock wrote to Sir James.[11] The Admiralty granted him a leave of absence and was generous with supplies. McClintock had expertise with steam, and during the searches he had developed and perfected sledging techniques. These proved to be exactly what was needed.

Early in 1859, eleven years, as they would learn, after the Franklin expedition abandoned their vessels, McClintock and his second-in-command, First Lieutenant William Hobson, set out on their epic journey. They left the *Fox* harboured at the eastern end of the dangerous waters of the Bellot Strait, which had been discovered during the searches, and with sledges and dogs travelled together towards King William Island, separating at Cape Victoria on the west coast of Boothia, with Hobson going north round King William Island to the west coast and McClintock south, first to the estuary of the Back River and then on up King William Island's west coast. In a cairn at Victory Point on the west side, Hobson was the first to find the vital record, the only official communication ever discovered: The *Erebus* and the *Terror* had been abandoned 22 April 1848, after having been beset in the ice northwest of King William Island for two winters. Sir John Franklin had died 11 June 1847, and in addition nine officers and fifteen men were also dead. Franklin's second-in-command, Captain Crozier, declared he was heading south with '105 souls' towards the mainland and the Great Fish River.

These snatches of information have occasioned endless speculation. Why did Crozier's men travel south rather than follow Sir John Ross's example and head north to Fury Beach, where they might have hoped for rescue by whalers? What accounted for the deaths of such a large proportion of officers in comparison with the men? At the time of abandonment, the expedition had already lost almost half of all its officers. With responsibility for 105 individuals – a little short of five times the number who retreated to Fury Beach with John Ross – Crozier faced formidable challenges. Fury Beach was a much closer objective than any Hudson's Bay Company post which might be reached some 1,200 miles away via the Back River, and there were still fairly large amounts of supplies at Fury Beach. In 1875, in a publication called *Smith's Arctic Expe-*

ditions, John Rae expressed his opinion: 'What struck me at the time, as it still does, was the great mistake made by Franklin's party in attempting to save themselves by retreating to the Hudson's Bay territories ... when the well-known route to Fury Beach – certainly much more accessible than any of the Hudson's Bay Company settlements, and by which the Rosses escaped in 1832–'33 – was open to them ... Had the retreat upon Fury Beach been resolved upon, the necessity for hauling heavy boats would have been avoided, for during the previous season (that of 1847) a small sledge party might have been dispatched thither to ascertain whether the provisions and boats at the depot were safe and available ...'[12] (Crozier may have been uncertain about the quantity and quality of these, and with his men in bad health and scurvy a factor, he undoubtedly knew he needed fresh meat. He may have reasoned that this would be easier obtained on the Back River, though to feed such a number of men from the land was probably an impossible task. Ice master Blanky could certainly have informed him that game was scarce in the Fury Beach area, although somewhat less so in the spring.) The reasons for Crozier's decisions can never be known; he may have hoped that a rescue operation would be sent down the Back River; this, the suggestion of irritating Dr King, had after all been done before. Apparently Crozier decided on his plan of action well ahead and planned his retreat carefully – he had the heavy lifeboats he took with him lightened and adapted for river travel.[13] They had, of course, to be mounted on heavy sledges – and, as it turned out, pulled by dying men.

In discussing the retreat from the vessels, Cyriax notes investigators have concluded some men would have been rescued if the expedition had headed for Fury Beach; and some might have survived if the Admiralty had dispatched at an early moment a rescue mission down the Back River.[14]

Much has been surmised, but it is Inuit who have told most of what is known of the expedition's tragic history. They told their stories to John Rae; to Leopold McClintock; to Americans Charles Francis Hall, who persisting after his enforced sojourn on Baffin Island, spent the years 1864–9 in Hudson Bay in hopes of rescuing survivors, and William H. Gilder of the Schwatka expedition (1878–80) in search of the Franklin records; to Norwegian Roald Amundsen during his historic transit of the passage (1903–6); and to Inuktitut-speaking Knud Rasmussen of the Danish Fifth Thule Expedition in 1923. These and stories still current today paint a dark picture of the expedition's progress south.

4 The Death Marches: 'They were seen carrying human meat'

Skeletons of Franklin's crews still turn up on the shores of King William Island. Tommy Anguttitauruq has found one himself. 'About twenty years ago my brother and I were goose hunting around Douglas Bay. We found a skeleton with a clay pipe still there and we thought at the time it might be one of the Franklin people. Six or seven years later, we think some researchers found the same skeleton with the clay pipe and a button under him. When I was out next in the area with my ATV, the skeleton was gone. Either that or I wasn't in the right place.'

King William Island is the lode source for Franklin stories, but you hear Franklin stories everywhere. This is because of hunting and migration patterns in traditional times and the modern-day move to the settlements. Inuit who met Franklin survivors on their death marches (Tommy's ancestors were among them) moved with the seasons from King William Island in search of game and took their stories with them. Wherever they were told, the stories created indelible impressions.

When I visit Gjoa Haven, Tommy Anguttitauruq is directing the community oral history program. 'Some of the old people still know the stories,' he says, 'but sometimes it is difficult to get the stories. Some of the old people say it is better not to talk too much. The white men cursed the land, they cursed it.'

Tommy shares with me some of the stories he has collected and tells me traditions passed down in his own family. Generations of his family and extended family have hunted on King William Island, and as a child he heard from his grandmother (his father's adopting mother), Agnes Aknayak Alikamick, who died in 1969, stories she herself had

The Franklin searches: *Loss of the McLellan* (1852).

heard from her own grandparents and other elders. ('She was old and blind and my grandfather was deaf. He used to call her "my little ears."') She passed on stories of two ships beset in the ice northwest of King William Island and of groups of white men straggling southward over the land. 'They were all scattered,' Tommy says. 'The way I heard it, some of the crews went down the east side and some of the crews went down the west side. The ones I heard of [from family members] went through the west side. They were all scattered and some of the people were disoriented – something like that.'[1]

Tommy has heard the stories of cannibalism and says, 'Even before this, some of them already didn't seem to be right. Some of the Inuit would try to help some of these white people who seemed not quite right, but they wouldn't want to receive help. They would grab and burst out screaming. So something didn't seem right to the Inuit, though of course we couldn't understand what they were saying.' Researchers have concluded that illness, certainly scurvy but very likely in combination with other disease – lead poisoning and botulism have been postulated – contributed to the tragedy. In contrast, Sir John Ross's crews, after four winters in the ice, had the energy to row as much as twenty miles in a day in pursuit of the whalers who eventually rescued them.

On their trek, the crews dropped as they walked. They died at death camps along the King William Island shore and died in numbers at Starvation Cove and also other points on the Adelaide Peninsula. Richard J. Cyriax concludes that as men died on the journey, members of the original party hived off and became smaller units. He suggests this began to happen at the time of the encampment at Terror Bay, when many men were by then too ill to continue and where it has been suggested a field hospital was set up.[2] What is uncertain is the date of the camp at Terror Bay. The traditional reconstruction of the fate of Franklin's crews has them struggling along the route to the Back River in 1848, but as we will see in chapter 5, new Inuit stories have come to light that suggest a later date, 1850, the date Inuit gave Rae as the year when white men in difficulties were sighted.

Encounters with hard-pressed crews have been preserved in the oral tradition. In 1999, Tommy Anguttitauruq heard the old shaman Nicholas Qayutinuaq, only shortly before his death, tell the story of Inuit meeting desperate white men on the south side of Terror Bay.[3] Tommy had Qayutinuaq tell the story three times:

'At this time there were four or five families with four or five separate igloos on the west side of King William Island to the south side of Terror Bay. The men were out seal hunting, and the women and children, and one elder too old to keep up with the younger men, were left in camp. At that time eight or nine white people came to the camp ...

'When the white men entered the camp, all the Inuit were inside one of the igloos; they started hearing people outside. One of the women says, "The hunters are here – they're back already." They didn't expect them back so soon. Then a woman went out to see them. She comes back very shaky and says, "They're not Inuit; they're not human." Everyone got scared, very, very scared and no one wanted to go outside. But the old man, when he hears something outside the igloo, he goes out to investigate – to see what's going on. When he sees what's outside, he says to himself, "No, I have never seen anything like this."

'He'd seen a shaman but he wasn't a shaman himself. He says to himself, "I've never in all my life seen a devil or a spirit. These things are not human; so if they are not human I cannot see them. I have never in all my life seen any kind of spirit – I've heard the sounds they make, but I've never seen them with my own eyes; these are not spirits."

'Then the old man goes over to touch one, to feel if it's cold or warm. He touched a cheek with his hand: cool but not as cold as a fish! They were beings but not Inuit. They were beings but he didn't know what they were.

'He had thought to himself, "If they are human, I can feel them. If they are human, they will be warm. If devils or spirits, they will have no heat." So he touched one and the being was cold – but not as cold as a fish! You know the fish is cold-blooded.

'These beings seemed disoriented – not too interested in the Inuit, more aware of the igloo building; touching it. The Inuk invited them inside and the women tried to give them something to eat – seal meat that was cooked already, and they gave them water to drink. They drank the water. But when they tried to give them seal meat, they'd take a bite and some of them swallowed; some of them wouldn't swallow, they'd spit it out. They gave them soup. Some drank a little; some didn't want to take any.

'Before the men came back, the old man instructed the women to bring these beings to one of the igloos – the biggest one. Then he walked to meet the hunters and told them what had been encountered; that there were strange beings in one of the igloos. They did not seem dangerous but they were "palakhonguliqtut" – getting weak, weak from hunger. The old man guided the hunters to the igloo where all the women and children were, so they could discuss.

'They had to be qallunaat, people thought – they had iron; guns and knives. In those days, iron was valuable and rare; you could sharpen it and make tools out of it or hunting equipment. These strange people had iron; they were probably qallunaat.

'The men decided to go and see them. These qallunaat were quite frightened when they saw the Inuit come in. But the men didn't harm them. They tried again to feed them with the cooked meat, but the qallunaat did the same thing as before – ate a little but not all.

'You hear people say sometimes that all Inuit eat raw meat. In the west when they're in their igloos, they like it cooked. So the Inuit started talking among themselves, saying if they come from the east they probably eat raw meat; we'd better try and see if they eat raw meat. So they gave them three whole seals. They built them an igloo and built a fire.

'Then the Inuit got together and talked to each other. They said, "We have heard that Indians kill Inuit. These could be Indians ... or white people. And we have also heard that qallunaat kill Inuit people sometimes. We'd better get going before they wake up."

'That night they got all their belongings together and took off towards the southwest. They never encountered those qallunaat again. But because they were in a hurry, they must have left a few of their belongings behind. Later that winter, two or three of them decided to go back to their old camp to gather up their possessions; they saw four dead bodies in that igloo. Originally there had been nine or ten white men. The seals were never touched; but two of the men were partly eaten; the other two must have been the last survivors.'

Tommy Anguttitauruq also collected a story about the retreating white men from the Gjoa Haven sculptor Nelson Takkiruq, who died in 1999 on Nunavut Day.[4] In this story, the group of Inuit who meet qallu-naat are further east than the former group, and they are seal hunting around the Ivory Islands. Tommy says this might be the same story Nicholas Qayutinuaq told, but passed on through a different family in a different manner:

'There were three or four families and the men were out seal hunting, south of the island and close to where they could see people coming to their camp. They rush home because they are afraid their women are being stolen by different people from the west or wherever different tribes might be coming from to steal their women. So they rush home and the people they met were quite strange. They noticed they were not Inuit, but they were not quite sure who they were. They tried to talk to them, but they made no sense. But they tried to talk to them; they were not afraid of them. They were afraid but not terrified. So they tried to talk to them, but they could not talk to them. They tried to trade with them, but these qallunaat wouldn't trade nothing. An Inuk asked for a knife and the white man just grabbed hold of it. The qallunaat wouldn't trade anything at all. The Inuit decided, "We better build them an igloo and we better give them some skins because their clothes are so wet." So they built them an igloo and they built themselves a little fire, but the smoke was terrible, so the Inuit said to themselves, "We'd better give them a kudluk so they can warm up. If they thank us we may get some-thing from them." They did that and they tried to feed them; the qallu-naat ate quite a bit. They also gave them two seals, so they could feed themselves. But that night the Inuit got together and took off and never went back.'

The shaman Nicholas Qayutinuaq also told his stepson Mark Tootiak about another encounter a group of Inuit had with more white men, this time further along on the route to the Back River. At the time he passed it on to me in an interview, he was Gjoa Haven's community constable.

'My stepfather was supposed to have been born in 1909, and accord-ing to him he heard these stories from his grandfather when he was a

Cold and Hungry, by Stanley Elongnak Klengenberg. Stencil on paper, printed by Elsie Klengenberg, Holman, 1986. 'The hunter has camped,' said Klengenberg of this work. 'He knows he must find game. His family and friends are waiting and are just as cold and hungry as he is.'

small boy. This group of Inuit was at a sealing camp in the month when the young seals are already born, hunting around the Etuk Islands off the Adelaide Peninsula, when they saw something black, a small group of people. Before they arrived, there was a shaman with the Inuit who said, "They are different people, they might be different people." The Inuit found out they were friendly and someone put up a small igloo for them. They gave them what they could, a little of what they could, because they didn't have much. One of the men was a big man and very friendly. He was hairy, they touched his skin and he had hair on his chest, a big man and friendly. After a few days they treated him specially – they gave him a woman. The Inuit were getting along well with the strangers and they might have stayed longer but they left – they themselves were so poor they could not take any of the strangers with them.

'Later, maybe a year later, these Inuit heard that people had seen more white people, a lot more white people, dying. They were seen carrying human meat, small pieces, because they were so hungry. They died on the morning side – where the sun comes up – of Richardson Point [Starvation Cove].'

Inuit who met Leopold McClintock on the sledging journey during which Crozier's record was discovered told him that the white men had been seen carrying skulls and also bones from legs and arms that appeared to be sawn off.

Scott Cookman, in his book *Ice Blink*, must certainly be right when he says the sight would have terrified the Inuit.[5] Who would be next? But Inuit have had to eat human flesh themselves, *in extremis*. 'I've heard such stories in connection with my own people,' says Cambridge Bay elder Moses Koihok.[6]

Some survivors appear to have reached the territory of the Back River people. Relics (some think they might have been from Inuit caches) were found on Montreal Island in Chantrey Inlet and, a short distance southeast, at the island known as Umiaktalik – 'the place of the boat' – which qallunaat call King Island. (An island called Umiaktalik appears on a map in *Schwatka's Search*.) Mark Tootiak says, 'There's a big wooden mast there you can see underground. My brother-in-law lifted it up and put one side on top of a rock. It's still there. My stepdad used to tell me that when he was young he found pieces of glass there.' And Mark once found a relic himself. 'I was looking around and I saw a big spike – old, old copper, all green with a square head.'

Tommy Anguttitauruq has hunted in the Chantrey Inlet area and knows the traditions of the people of the Back River. He and his brother Michael found old sledge runners there, which they thought came from the expedition, and his brother fixed them up and used them for years. 'The Back River people in the springtime, in March, April, and May and probably also in June, would go to the Chantrey Inlet area, near the Montreal Island, and around the area they found a lifeboat – I heard only one boat; I'm not sure if there was one boat or two. There were no people around it. Those Back River people used anything they could to break it up. They made all kinds of holes with rocks and broke up the boat as much as they could so the white people wouldn't be able to use it to attack them. They thought the white people were planning to attack – they thought they were hiding somewhere in the area. They were afraid of them. After a few years those boats were still there, so they started taking them apart in order to use the nails and the piece of steel on the bottom – the keel. That piece of steel they pounded up to make harpoons and spears.'

These people had never seen white people, Tommy says, but they had heard stories that caused them great fear. They had heard from Inuit on Baffin Island how two white people in the eastern Baffin region had killed two hunters sleeping under their kayaks. 'The white people killed them without waking them up. There was one survivor who escaped. As he ran off there was a big bang but he didn't get hit. At the time they didn't know about guns, but that was a gun. So these Inuit in the Chantrey Inlet area figured every white person was dangerous – too dangerous.'[7]

Mark Tootiak remembers how when he was a little boy on fishing trips to the Back River, his stepfather Nicholas Qayutinuaq always pointed out to him a great crack in the granite mountain at Qijuktakvik – 'the place to gather heather.' 'We'd see the crack below the rapids when we went fishing. He said that in that crack there are human bones. Therefore it is taboo. It is forbidden to go there and disturb the bones. I was five or so when I first heard the story, and my stepfather would repeat it every time we were in the area.'

There are undoubtedly animal bones in the crack. Are there human bones as well? How would Mark Tootiak feel if someone investigated the crack today? 'You know, my son and I talk about it a lot. We could go there with some good strong ropes.' His stepfather never said whose bones they were, only that they were human bones, and up until now, as far as he knows, no one has been inside the crack. 'There's a feeling "better safe than sorry."' And how does he think the bones got there? 'I have often wondered.' The story, he says, is 'part of the information that has been passed on.'[8]

Did some members of the Franklin expedition come to a violent end in the hands of Inuit? The Central Arctic world was by no means a peaceable kingdom. Within Inuit society, blood feuds and revenge murder were the order of the day. While the Parry and Ross expeditions established good relations with Inuit, there were flashpoints that could have led to violence. The Back expedition left Inuit dead. Cyriax notes that some Inuit who met Dr Rae in 1854, at the time he heard the first reports of the Franklin tragedy, 'tried to lead him astray' and seemed opposed to his travelling west towards King William Island. Leopold McClintock met terror-stricken Inuit who 'would give him no information,' and 'Colonel Gilder [of the Schwatka expedition] believed that certain Eskimos would gladly have killed him and other members of his party in order to obtain their equipment.'[9]

In 1850, near the start of the Franklin searches, the possibility that some of Franklin's crew had perished in hostile action received considerable attention after Adam Beck, a Greenlandic Inuit interpreter employed by Sir John Ross, reported to British naval officers that he had been told by natives of the wrecks of two ships and a massacre of white men who had among them men who wore epaulettes. His stories indicated that a part of the crews from the ships drowned, and that the remainder 'were some time in huts or tents apart from the natives, that they had guns but no balls ...' and were killed by darts and arrows. Much confusion attended the tale (and its interpretation), particularly with regard to the location of the action, a place referred to as Omanek, a common name used widely. The story was dismissed as wilful fabrication and its teller ridiculed, although Adam Beck made a legal declaration that he had passed on only what he had been told.[10] Charles Francis Hall, when he met him, believed him.[11]

It is possible to find echoes of the Franklin tragedy in Adam Beck's story. As we will learn, there are Inuit traditions that say some of Franklin's crews died by drowning, and among Adam Beck's statements is a reference to 'a stone cairn under which bodies had been buried.' A violent incident accounting for the deaths of a few Franklin men cannot be ruled out, but no evidence has come to light to support one.

Crozier's last words to the outside world were that he had with him '105 souls.' Searchers have found skeletons all along the route of the journey to the Back River, many at resting places that became death camps. More bodies must have been washed away by the ocean as, in the opinion of researchers, parties with boats on heavy sledges would travel along the ice whenever possible and would camp close to shore. However, investigators have usually put the number of skeletons recovered along the known route of the death march at less than fifty. Were there other routes that Franklin's men took to death?

5 New Franklin Stories: The Ship at Imnguyaaluk

The Royal Geographical Society Islands were officially added to the maps only after the Northwest Passsage was accomplished. Amundsen discovered and mapped them and named them after one of his sponsors. But Inuit have always gone to the Royal Geographical Society Islands – and still do – for the bearded seal in the springtime, and to the northern parts – 'where there is often blood on the ground' – for polar bear hunting. In interviews with elders of the Kitikmeot Heritage Society in Cambridge Bay, I learn that a tradition exists – fading but still extant – that an exploring vessel wintered in these islands.

The wrecks of the *Erebus* and the *Terror* have never been found and for students of the Franklin tragedy the great mysteries concern the vessels. What happened to the ships?

The last official position of Franklin's vessels, according to the record discovered in the cairn at Victory Point, has them beset in the ice northwest of King William Island. At the time of abandonment, they had apparently worked their way a few miles south from their position the previous year. On his way north up the west coast of King William Island to the cairn where the record was found, Leopold McClintock came upon a lifeboat left on the shore in which were two bodies. The boat was pointing north, as if being dragged back to the abandoned ships. This and stories he heard from the Inuit convinced him that one or both of the ships had been remanned (newest stories suggest by considerable numbers) and, released from the ice, had been navigated or had drifted to new positions. Most investigators have subscribed to this belief.

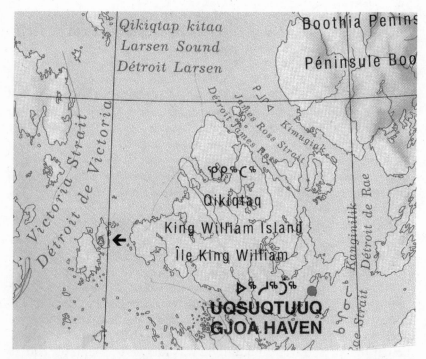

Arrow indicates pencil mark made by Frank Analok indicating the location of Imnguyaaluk, where, according to the oral tradition, an exploring ship wintered.

The Ship at Imnguyaaluk

Frank Analok, honorary chair, Moses Koihok, Mabel Angulalik, and I sit around a table in the coffee shop of the Arctic Islands Lodge. Michael Kanayuk has brought us together, and we have James Pamioyok to interpret. Jessie Hakungak brings us plenty of refills of coffee. The Cambridge Bay elders are cautious and careful in their comments. Shipwrecks figured in the stories of their childhood, and now they wish they could remember more. ('Little did they know it was going to be something big,' remarks interpreter James Pamioyok.)

Frank Analok puts a mark on our Arctic map to indicate the locale of his story – Imnguyaaluk, an island called after a shaman who died there, they say, before white men came to the North. His mark falls

squarely on the south coast of the upper island in the Royal Geographical Society group. Frank says he first heard the story from Patsy Topilikton, an elder who died some years ago.

'Our ancestors have told us that an expedition ship wintered on this
island,' he begins. 'One of the first ships that came around wintered
here. The Inuit who have long passed on before us knew about the
white men being there, but our generation has only heard the stories.

'I heard from Patsy where the place was where they actually wintered. According to Patsy they were iced in and had no choice. During
their time at Imnguyaaluk, they made use of seal oil and blubber – there
are large traces of seal oil on the ground. They must have heated things
right on the surface of the land. When there's a concentration of oil, it
leaves a slick.

'One time, many years later, some Inuit were there on this island –
next to the bigger one – waiting for the ice to go, waiting for the ice to
melt. And when the ice melted, they found the seal-oil slick.

'According to our ancestors there had been quite a few white men. I
don't know how many but there was a man called Meetik – duck – and
a person who was talked about a lot, who was superior. Inuit called him
in Inuktitut "Qoitoyok" – "the one who goes to the bathroom a lot," an
older man called Qoitoyok – "he who goes to the bathroom a lot."' Even
though this person was an adult, he was known to pee in his bed at
night. That's just the way he was.

'The Inuit probably visited the white men because they were the first
to try to come through. The white man showed some papers ...'

Might the papers have been maps? Were the white men asking for
help? Frank cannot specify what the papers were. Did the Inuit go
aboard the ship? 'Maybe they weren't allowed to,' says Frank.

'The Inuit may have helped the white men to keep themselves shel-
tered and to keep themselves warm. They may have asked for help in
terms of providing food. They may have been shown polar bear hides
and have traded for sealskins.

'It has been said that once summer came the ship – with sails, like
flags – that wintered left for where we do not know, but perhaps for
wherever they had come from, and it is believed all the men left with
the ship. Whether they made it, I do not know.

'As a young man I went seal hunting before freeze-up in this place.
But we didn't see the oil slick because the ground was covered over. We
didn't find relics of the ship that wintered, but perhaps our ancestors
did. These people stayed on the island: that is proved by the fact that

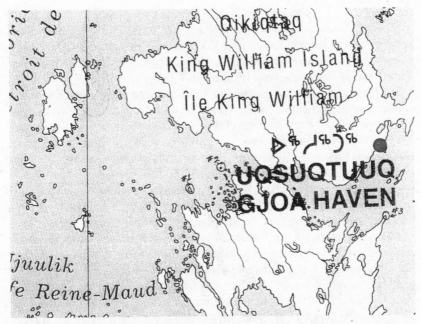

Michael Angottitauruq indicates by the numbers 1, 2, and 3 the locations where he saw oil slicks or fireplaces used for heat and cooking. The numerals indicate (1) Aveomavik, (2) Enogeiaqtuq, and (3) Seogaqtook – Ogle Point.

the ground is soiled by the rendered seal oil blubber. These people who stayed on the island used the seal oil for heat.'

The Fireplace Trail

Oil slicks that appear to be similar to the oil slick Frank Analok refers to have been sighted in other places fairly recently. While out hunting, perhaps around 1984, Michael Angottitauruq, Tommy's brother (the brothers spell their last name slightly differently), the president of the Kitikmeot Wildlife Board, a former mayor of Gjoa Haven, and also, before the creation of Nunavut, a twice-elected member of the Legislative Assembly of the Northwest Territories, came across such a slick at an island called Aveomavik ('place of joyful cheers'), which lies among the many islands off the coast of the Adelaide Peninsula mainland. He was duck hunting with his son, and it was his son who was the first to see the oil slick, alerting him to the remains of a campfire which, he says, would never have been made by Inuit. This caused him to look around, and he says, 'I found a skull and bones, possibly the remains of three people. They didn't look like Inuit dead. They didn't have any rocks around them, the way Inuit used to bury their dead.'

The thought occurred to him at the time that these skeleton parts could have come from victims of the Franklin disaster. A few years previously when out with his four children – 'I like them to know the land' – he had, in fact, seen a number of other oil slicks at another island in the group, this one called Enogeiaqtuq ('where there are lots of people'). One of the children was again the first to point out a strange oil slick, and this time Michael noticed a number of slicks. A son dug up one (he later put it back) so there could be closer examination, and Michael believes there can be no other explanation than that they were made by white men.[1] 'The oil slicks were deeply into the sand. Oil does not evaporate. They were not made by Inuit; Inuit don't use oil that way. The people who made them had used them for cooking, possibly for heating, which could be why they were so deep into the sand. They were approximately two feet wide in diameter and a foot and a half deep into the sand. They were very old. They were the colour of sand but darker because the seal oil had dripped and seeped into them. [See illustration drawn by Michael Angottitauruq.] When cooking, the qallunaat would have used them with some other implement. Because of the way they were made, the people who did them would not have been just passing through, but there for some days at least.'

The only time the oil slicks would be visible on the ground is at the end of July and beginning of August, and in mid-summer 2006, Michael Angottitauruq decided to visit Enogeiaqtuq again to take a closer look. This time he concluded, after inspection, that the site is later than the Aveomavik site. He counted nine oil slicks, but only one of these he thinks was used for cooking. 'I found the others seemed to be places to keep warm.' He theorizes that possibly tents could have been held down around them with tent pegs. He believes this camp might have been used by people investigating the Franklin disaster. 'This camp had to be made by people in good physical condition.'

In his travels, Michael has also come upon another oil slick site – the most puzzling he says. 'This is further east along the Simpson Strait at Ogle Point – Seogaqtook ["full of sand"] – and was right on the shore where the water reaches it. It was quite large so it make me think and believe it had been a signal and warming fire in winter.'

Top View, Looking from above ground
from standing position. They are all on
Sandy Ground. All I studied closely are
bout 1½ Foot to 2 Feet diamaters round. Closer
study may find larger sizes

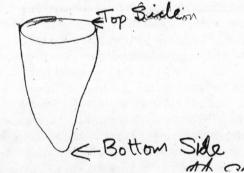

← 1 ½ Foot →
OR
2 Feet

I dug   one out of the ground to see
how deep it may have gone into the ground.
Sand was glued together by the oil

←Top Side

Top Side

←Bottom Side

.128

'Top view: looking from above ground from standing position. They are all on sandy ground. All nine studied closely are about 1.5 feet to 2 feet diameters round. Closer study may find larger sizes.'

'Dug one out of the ground to see how deep it may have gone into the ground. Sand was glued together by the oil.' Sketch by Michael Angottitauruq.

Michael Angottitauruq thinks all the sites have a connection of some sort to the Franklin disaster. The camp at Enogeiaqtuq seems to have the earmarks perhaps of an official search party. 'Yes, I was surprised when I saw the slicks.' he says, 'but I had heard that a ship had wintered in the islands. Old people now dead had known that.'

Tommy Anguttitauruq also provides a story relating to a ship that wintered. In this story, the great metal wealth of the qallunaat appears to have given rise to provocative action. Tommy says the story originally came from Simon Qirqut, the King William Island elder who had a store of Franklin stories which he passed on to his sons.

'In the later winter when the days were getting longer, the Inuit were seal hunting and they found people on a ship. This was way before Inuit in this region knew anything about white people. They didn't know who these people were, what race they were – they only knew they were human. These Inuit people started taking stuff out of the ship – taking out metal and wood, anything they could put their hands on – while the ship was unable to leave. The white people didn't do anything, just watched. Maybe there were too many of these Inuit people – or maybe they were aggressive. We don't know who these people were – whether they were Netsilikmuit from Boothia or King William Island, Keelenikmuit from Victoria Island, or Iluiliqmuit from the Queen Maud Gulf mainland.'

Tommy believes it likely this encounter occurred somewhere in the vicinity of the islands where his brother Michael saw the oil slicks.

In the light of these stories, the question arises: do they relate to Franklin's men and to one or both of the vessels? The oil slicks lead to Ogle Point at Chantrey Inlet, the entry to the mouth of the Back River, the objective of the Franklin crews on their death march. The odds seem overwhelming that these stories extend our knowledge of the expedition's end – while giving rise to many questions. According to Frank Analok's story, the ship in the Royal Geographical Society Islands left at break-up with all the men aboard her. It is possible to reconstruct the fate of the ship at Imnguyaaluk in the following manner: after negotiating the many shoals in the area, she arrived among the many islands off the Adelaide Peninsula. Was the ship damaged by ice and did her crews camp on Aveomavik, Enogeiaqtuq, and perhaps other islands? Were the crews low in ammunition, and did Inuit board their vessel without opposition or warning shots fired? Did the crews eventually take ship's boats and set out for the Back River, from time to time putting up tiny tents that Tommy Anguttitauruq describes as 'like envelopes set upside down'? This would solve one Franklin mystery since it indicates some crew members tried to reach the Back River as late as 1850. This was the year the first reports received by Dr John Rae indicated Inuit sighted white men who had lost their ships. This date has puzzled investigators, as the official record found by the McClintock expedition gives the date of abandonment of the vessels and the start of the trek to the Back River as 1848. The wintering of a Franklin ship at Imnguyaaluk also solves another mystery. Among the stories told to Charles Francis Hall, several mention visits to an exploring ship frozen in the ice. These stories seemed improbable to researchers: Inuit did not apparently find the boats and the valuable supplies left on shore at the time of the abandonment of Franklin's vessels until after they were found by the McClintock expedition. This suggested the Inuit had no knowledge of the vessels. But Inuit did visit the ship at Imnguyaaluk and gave Inuit names – still remembered – to at least two of the people they met: Meetik – duck – and Qoitoyok – 'the great pisser,' as interpreter James Pamioyok put it. ('They called him this because he was sick,' says Tommy Anguttitauruq. Until recent times, and perhaps sometimes still, Inuit customarily gave visitors Inuit names – usually because of physical characteristics or the work they did.)

According to the Inuit

What was the fate of this vessel navigated to the islands off the coast of the Adelaide Peninsula and boarded and looted by Inuit in what the story Tommy Anguttitauruq recounts, suggests may have been an abrasive action? Stories of Inuit sinking a ship appear both in Inuit oral history and in perhaps rather milder manner in the searchers' written records.

'In the 1800s they were exploring the land up here – pushing towards the east. But they couldn't succeed – because of the ice ... A ship sank somewhere. I can't tell you where; there were no communities in those days, but a ship sank somewhere,' says Moses Koihok. 'When one of the first ships came up here, I've heard that the Inuit didn't want to have anything to do with the people. In those years the Inuit were well off from the land and they were leery, cautious to accept them. They weren't given reason to fear them, they were not given cause; they really didn't have any problem with them. But they were intruding on the Inuit land, and I've heard that the Inuit sank the ship. The Inuit had no idea why the first explorers were coming onto their land and they were afraid. Perhaps they decided the best thing was to sink their ship ... The shamans may have played a role. They were protectors in the old days.'

Frank Analok says, 'Yes, I've heard the stories about Inuit sinking ships. My stepfather told of a premeditated incident. Because Inuit were afraid of the unknown, they may have sunk the ship. The shamans may have played a role. Because they were shamans, they were able to do this. The Inuit were afraid of the white men – of the way they approached, of the language the Inuit didn't understand – and because of this, they looked to the shaman to deal with these strangers.'

The Searchers' Stories

Leopold McClintock was the first searcher to hear news of the ships, and he heard it during two encounters with Inuit of the Boothia Peninsula. The information was given reluctantly. At their first meeting, his principal informant, 'Old Oonalee,' revealed only that Inuit knew of a ship that had sunk, but the second meeting was more productive, it seems, because there was a young man with the group who let the cat out of the bag.

'After much anxious enquiry we learned that two ships had been seen by the natives of King William's Island; one of these was seen to sink in deep water, and nothing was obtained from her, a circumstance at which they expressed much regret; but the other was forced on shore by the ice, where they suppose she still remains, but is much broken. From this ship they have obtained most of their wood, etc.; and Oot-loo-lik is the name of the place where she grounded ... Old Oonalee, who drew the rough chart for me in March, to show where the ship sank, now answered our questions respecting the one forced on shore, not a syllable about her did he mention on the former occasion, although we asked whether they knew of only one ship? I think he would willingly have kept us in ignorance of the wreck being upon the coast, and the young man unwittingly made it known to us.

'The latter also told that the body of a man was found on board ship: that he must have been a very large man, and had long teeth.'[2]

McClintock understood Oot-loo-lik, where the Inuit said the ship grounded, to be on the west coast of King William Island. The word gave rise to confusion. Later investigators thought Inuit stories placed Oot-loo-lik south of King William Island and identified it, in turn, as O'Reilly Island and Grant Point on the Adelaide Peninsula, part of the North American mainland. However, the late veteran HBC trader and fluent Inuktitut speaker L.A. Learmonth pointed out in the 1969 spring issue of *The Beaver* that Oot-loo-lik refers not to any one point but to an area (which includes all these points) where 'Oogeook' – uguk, bearded seal – are plentiful and much hunted by Inuit over the ice in the spring.[3] Tommy Anguttitauruq describes this hunting ground as an immense region which includes the Royal Geographical Society Islands (added to the maps only in the twentieth century by Roald Amundsen) and extends south from the western coast of King William Island to the coast of the Adelaide Peninsula and North American mainland, and west to the east coast of Jenny Lind Island. On modern bilingual maps of Nunavut, the area is shown reaching the coast of Queen Maud Gulf.

Hall was the next after McClintock to hear the story, and he heard it from the same group of Inuit – the Netsilik from the Boothia Peninsula – as McClintock. He talked to them when he came upon their camp of snow houses on the sea ice as he was nearing King William Island: 'A native of the island first saw the ship when sealing; it was far off seaward, beset in the ice. He concluded to make his way to it, though at first he felt afraid; got aboard but saw no one, although from every appearance somebody had been living there. At last he ventured to steal a knife, and made off as fast as he could to his home; but on showing the Innuits what he had stolen the men of the place all started off for the ship. To get into the igloo (cabin) they knocked a hole through because it was locked. They found there a dead man, whose body was very large and heavy, his teeth very long ... He was left where they found him. One place in the ship where a great many things were found was very dark; they had to find things there by feeling around. Guns were there and a great many very good buckets and boxes ... From time to time the Neitchilles [*sic*] went to get out of her whatever they could; they made their plunder into piles on board, intending to sledge it to their igloos some time after; but on going again they found her sunk, except the top of the masts. They said they had made a hole in her bottom by getting out one of her timbers or planks. The ship was afterwards much broken up by the ice, and the masts, timbers, boxes, casks, etc drifted on shore.'[4]

Hall was later told by one of his informants that one side of the ship had been damaged by ice. 'The Innuits saw that nearly the whole side of one side of the vessel had been crushed in by the heavy ice that was about it, and thought that was why the Kob-lu-nas had left it and gone to the land and lived in the tents. By and by the Kob-lu-nas froze and starved.'[5]

Much magnified detail from an Inuit map drawn for whaling captain George Comer by Teseuke – Harry – his whaling mate. Both C.F. Hall and Lt Fredrick Schwatka led Franklin searches with the aid of guides and dog-team drivers recruited from the Repulse Bay area.

Ten years later, Gilder heard the first eye-witness account. Ikinnelik-patolok had been to the vessel himself: 'We learned at the interview that he had only once seen white men alive. That was when he was a little boy ... He was fishing on Back's River when they came along in a boat and shook hands with him. [Probably the Back expedition.] The next white man he saw was dead in a bunk of a big ship which was frozen in the ice near an island about five miles due west of Grant Point, on Adelaide Peninsula. They had to walk out about three miles on smooth ice to reach the ship ... About this time he saw the tracks of white men on the main-land. When he first saw them there were four, and afterward only three. This was when the spring snows were falling. When his people saw the ship so long without anyone around, they used to go on board and steal pieces of wood and iron. They did not know how to get inside by the doors, and cut a hole in the side of the ship, on a level with the ice, so that when the ice broke up during the following summer the ship filled and sunk. No tracks were seen in the salt-water ice or on the ship, which also was covered with snow, but they saw scrapings and sweepings alongside, which seemed to have been brushed off by people who had been living on board. They found some red cans of fresh meat, with plenty of what looked like tallow mixed with it. A great many had been opened, and four were still unopened. They saw no bread. They found plenty of knives, forks, spoons, pans, cups, and plates on board, and afterwards found a few things on shore after the vessel had gone down. They also saw books on board, and left them there. They only took knives, forks, spoons, and pans; the other things they had no use for.'[6]

There are more stories of Inuit boarding a ship, but not necessarily the same ship.

In 1905, Roald Amundsen met Inuit who said that Inuit had once found an unmanned vessel off Cape Crozier, the most western point of King William Island, and directly opposite the Royal Geographical Society Islands. These Inuit had entered her and some ate food from tins they found lying around, which made them ill and caused some to die. Amundsen considered the vessel might have eventually drifted and sunk north of the Royal Geographical Society Islands.[7]

In 1923, Rasmussen heard a story, perhaps over time adulterated by blended oral history, because in this story there is not one dead man on board but many. (As we will see, there are stories that suggest these dead may be symbolic figures.) And the locale appears to have been 'northwest of Qeqertaq – King William Island.' The story was told to Rasmussen by Qaqortingneq, who relates that two brothers were out sealing in the spring at the time when the snow melts away from the breathing holes: 'Far out on the ice they saw something black, a large black mass that could be no animal. They looked more closely and found it was a great ship ... At first they could not go down into the ship itself, but soon they became bolder and even ventured into the houses that were on deck. There they found many dead men lying in their bunks. At last they also risked going down into the enormous room in the middle of the ship. It was dark there. But soon they found tools and would make a hole in order to let light in. And the foolish people, not understanding white man's things, hewed a hole just on the water line so that the water poured in and the ship sank ... And it went to the bottom with all the valuable things, of which they barely rescued any.'[8]

In all, Inuit told five early investigators that they had boarded a ship and in three cases took the blame for sinking her.

The story in various forms is still alive in Gjoa Haven. In 1999 I recorded a version given to me by Matthew Tiringaneak, who in camp days hunted in the Back River area. This variation has been passed down in his family. In Tiringaneak's story, rather than a dead man there is a living person on board. (One of Hall's informants also said that while watching the ship in the ice in Oot-loo-lik he had seen a live man.)[9]

'There was a man out hunting who found a ship in the ice. He stayed outside it for a while and nobody seemed to be around. So he went back home and told people what he had found while out camping – a ship that was anchored and frozen in the ice. Three people decided to go over and see it next day and so the three of them went. By the time they arrived, it had already gotten dark – so dark that they could not see each other. But they decided they'd go inside, although it was very dark, and decided that every time they touched each other, they'd say, "Uvunga!" – "it's me!" They went inside and each time they grabbed one another, they said, "Uvunga," – "it's me!" Then somebody grabbed somebody and that person didn't "Uvunga!" He didn't say a word. One of the three Inuit said, "I've got somebody here."

'Before they went into the ship, they had all agreed: "If we touch a person and he's not one of us, we'll take him outside and see who he is." So when one of them yelled, "I have someone here," the other two went to try to help him take him outside. But this person started wrestling and trying to get away; they grabbed hold of him, but he got away. He went out of the boat and started running. They ran after him but he ran very fast towards Montreal Island and they never caught up with him. This ship was in the middle of the ocean and sank somewhere there.'

Since the days of the early searchers, numbers of expeditions have looked for the ship that Inuit boarded and that grounded at Oot-loo-lik. Recent investigations have had the advantage of state-of-the-art technology, but no discovery has been made.

The Second Ship

The stories told by Inuit say a ship came to her end in Oot-loo-lik after she had been boarded by the Inuit. What of the second ship?

Investigators have tended to believe that both vessels drifted or were navigated down the west coast of King William Island – certainly a valid line of investigation – but on King William Island, among some Inuit, another tradition exists. Tommy Anguttitauruq told me the account passed down in his family. Tommy says: 'My grandmother heard the story that one ship sank off northwest of King William Island, but the other ship went further northeast and disappeared. They tried to return the way they came from – not exactly the way they came, but when the ship wrecked the other ship tried to travel northeast around to the other side of the island. Whether this was Franklin's ship or the other ship, I don't know. Nobody ever really knew what happened.'

At first contact, Inuit called the explorers' ships 'floating islands,' because of their size and their wood and their masts. Tommy remembers that when he was a child, his grandmother used to like to hum to him an aye aye aye song about a ship: 'When we were sad, happy, we made up songs. This is an Aivilik song, but when my grandmother sang this song to me, she sang it as if the ship was going north round the island below us.

Ayayayaya Ayayaya Ayayaya
There's an island down below
It has tall posts and, sadly,
It is leaving through the channel
In direction of the current.
Ayayaya Ayayaya Ayayaya
There's an island down below
Unfortunately it's travelling
Southeast over there.
Ayayaya, Ayayaya, Ayayaya[10]

Researchers to date do not appear to have given much consideration to the possibility that a Franklin vessel may have attempted a retreat to the north (and which might have ended on the east side of King William Island). However, in 1931 Major L.T. Burwash of the Canadian Department of the Interior published startling information. Burwash, in three separate expeditions for the Canadian government between 1925 and 1930, had conducted investigations into many aspects of Arctic conditions – natural resources, Inuit health and welfare, the fur trade – and also into the Franklin tragedy. In a government publication entitled *Canada's Western Arctic*, he wrote that from what Inuit told him 'one is drawn to the conclusion that the ultimate fate of the Franklin party differed materially from that ordinarily pictured.'[11]

Burwash reported he had learned from several different native sources that Inuit had known for many years that 'the wreck of a large vessel lay submerged off the northeastern extremity [a small island] of Matty Island.' He concluded this was either the *Erebus* or the *Terror*, and that the vessel must have drifted through Simpson Strait, between King William Island and the Adelaide Peninsula, eastward to the vicinity of Matty Island.

Burwash's informants were Netsilik Inuit. He visited them at their snow sealing village on the ice between King William Island and the Boothia Peninsula on a sledging trip he made in March with two guides, Angnowya and Angote, two sledges, and nineteen dogs: 'Finally at 3 p.m. of the 12th the village of the seal hunters was reached. Here we found fifteen large igloos which housed the greater part of the Netselingmeut tribe. We were welcomed in the true Netselingmeut manner, the men first standing in a group at some little distance while the women of the settlement, who were mothers, each with a knife in her hand ran around our loaded sleds in a wide circle. According to their belief the track left by the women would encompass any evil spirits that had followed us across the ice, thus keeping them out of their settlement ... During the evenings as many as could crowd into our quarters presented themselves and were made happy with tobacco, their contribution of the evening being tales of the country and its people. From these people I learned much of the ship which is reported as lying under water on a reef off the east coast of Matty island and which can scarcely be any other than one of those abandoned by the Franklin party. They all agree as to its location and appearance and state that the coastline in its vicinity has long been productive of both iron and wood.'

Several years after the publication in 1931 of the Burwash findings, Chief Trader William (Paddy) Gibson, who had himself carried out a search of King William's south coast (though apparently not the east) and located and buried human remains, published in a special issue of the Hudson's Bay Company magazine *The Beaver* a lengthy informative article giving an overview of the Franklin disaster and all the literature it had engendered (no light task). In it, he rejects Burwash's reports of a sunken vessel in the Matty Island area. 'Prudent investigation will reveal that the report has no foundation in reality ...'[12]

A major reason for Gibson's dismissal of the report was that in it Burwash discusses a cache which Gibson correctly points out was left not by any of Franklin's men but by Roald Amundsen in 1903 on the first stretch of his transit of the Northwest Passage. Amundsen jettisoned two lots of deck cargo in an effort to lighten his ship when she grounded between tides in the waters around the Matty Islands. When safely through, he navigated over to the coast of Boothia and built a cairn.

Tommy's grandmother was there as a child with the group of Inuit who actually uncovered Amundsen's large supply depot: 'My grandmother was travelling with a group of people in the spring and summer. She told me she was a child or a teen. They were travelling to go seal hunting and they came upon this cache in the Matty Islands area. Local people say it was on Blenky Island. She was actually there when they uncovered the cache. There were burlap and cotton bags filled with flour and sugar and perhaps something like porridge – oatmeal. These were all buried in a mound covered with part of a cotton sail buried under sand and rocks – something the size of a tupik – an Inuit tent ring – and covered with rocks and then sand – quite thick – and when they uncovered this cache they found cans, sacks of sugar, oatmeal – "kind of flaky" – was the way she described it.

'They didn't know what the things were – what they were used for – so they emptied them out so they could use the burlap and cotton bags. They were all having fun – laughing, seeing the flour and the sugar blowing in the air. They said, "We have made a new kind of snow," and the children shook out the oatmeal and said, "We have made a new kind of raindrops!"'

Tommy remarks that these Inuit opened up the cans too, but they were all corroded and they dumped the contents, which smelled bad. But the metal was precious, and Tommy drew little pictures for me in my notebook showing how they 'put tiny strips of metal around the cutting edges of their ulus and weapons, fastening them on with bone rivets.'

As to the date of the cache, Tommy says his grandmother knew the cache was found the same year Amundsen's vessel arrived at Gjoa Haven – 1903.

Across on the Boothia coast lies a point Inuit have long known as Haviktalik – 'the place having metal.' This place got its name, Inuit elders say, long before Amundsen made his journey. Tommy explains, 'Right across from Haviktalik – this beach for finding metal – there's an island where Amundsen left some stuff. But it [the wreck] happened many years before Amundsen. That's why people from that area had bits and pieces of metal. They used the metal for harpoon heads and spears and made small ice chisels out of them. And it was not just tin cans but good-sized metal.' Tommy identified Haviktalik as being on the western shore of the Boothia Peninsula opposite the Matty Islands. For many years, the Inuit were grateful for what they found there. He speculates that the copper and steel found at 'the place having metal' could have come from the Franklin expedition 'because those people from the Franklin expedition went all over the place.'

In his report, Burwash writes, 'Before the time of the finding of the cache on the island the natives had frequently found wood (which from their description consisted of barrel staves) and thin iron (apparently barrel hoops) at various points along the coastlines in this area.'

While Tommy locates Haviktalik – the place having metal – as being on the shore of the Boothia Peninsula across from the Matty Islands, according to early Inuit testimony there was also a store of wreckage lower down the coast. David Woodman, who reviewed all the information collected by the early searchers in his book *Unravelling the Franklin Mystery*, locates it in the area of Cape Colville. Here he writes wreckage from the Oot-loo-lik ship had 'accumulated.' 'In 1869 Hall found that much of the wood from the Franklin wreck had been cached nearby, including a piece of ship's mast fourteen feet long, a box used for rope, two new native boats which had been made from the ship's mast and parts of ship's blocks.'[13] But was this wreckage from the Oot-loo-lik ship? And if so, where had she sunk?

The Case for a Ship

Pat Lyall, the Taloyoak businessman and former chairman of Nunasi, the Inuit-owned birthright corporation, has been keeping an eye out, and making occasional searches, for a Franklin vessel in waters around the Matty Islands for forty years. 'People seem to think a wreck might lie in Josephine Bay, perhaps thirty miles northeast of the Matty Islands. We think it could have drifted in there. There have been a number of sightings. People have spotted a mast and a greenish mass under the waters.'

Lyall believes it entirely likely that one of the Franklin vessels might have sailed north round King William Island and come to grief in the Matty Island area. He rejects the idea that confused tales – blended oral history – of the final end of Ross's *Victory* – carried away by the ice, she sank close to a small island, and for many years the top of her mast was visible – have led to stories of a wreck near the Matty Islands. 'That's completely different,' he says.

Long-time Taloyoak resident and retired HBC trader Alex Buchan says, 'Reports of a sunken vessel in the area have been persistent.'

Knud Rasmussen is known to have expressed the opinion that the key to the Franklin mystery might lie on the east side of King William

Island. An old Arctic hand who met Rasmussen in his later travels declared, 'Rasmussen, after years of study and delving into the history of the Huskies [Inuit] had arrived at the one way to make a successful hunt ... You see how all the parties concentrated on the west. Look, they even went down as far as the mainland of Canada. But every one of them was on the wrong trail according to Rasmussen and I believe he had the right dope ...'[14] Tommy Anguttitauruq's relatives were Rasmussen's helpers while he visited King William Island. 'He built a small shack about thirty-five miles from Gjoa Haven, I guess to the west, where some people go fishing sometimes. My grandfather was hunting for him and my grandmother was preparing clothing for him.' Tommy's grandparents likely passed on to Rasmussen the same information Tommy can still impart today. But wherever the Franklin ships now lie, Rasmussen believed, they 'were crushed by the ice, even if at first they were found by the Eskimos, still undamaged, but abandoned by their crews.'[15] Rasmussen thought this to be a certainty because the Inuit got so little from them; they had silver spoons and other small relics in their possession, but very little of the wood and metal that were truly valuable to them. In contrast, John Ross's *Victory* supplied wealth for more than a hundred years to Boothia Inuit and through inter-Inuit trade to others farther away.

In interviews, three famous elders supplied stories supporting the case for a ship and the deaths of white men to the east of King William Island.

Rosie Iqallijuq of Igloolik had a dramatic story to tell: ' I heard from the elder Kuuttiq [of Cambridge Bay][16] that white people died in a ship lost between Taloyoak and Gjoa Haven. Kuuttiq was frequenting between Gjoa Haven, Taloyoak, and Cambridge Bay and he told me about these people. Apparently there is a very strong current between Gjoa Haven and Taloyoak. The story I heard was that the ship was making an effort to avoid ice, and because of the current the ship got into the thick of the ice and began to break – with the consequence that the crew died. Some of the crew died right away; some survived. I even heard that one crew member was dismembered.'

Bibian Neeveeovak, of Taloyoak, remembers stories from her childhood: 'When I was young, I heard of a couple of wrecks. The white people from the wrecks starved. In the cold ... At the time when I was young, I wasn't paying much attention. Now, being older, I'm starting to forget what I heard before. White men long ago starved around Matty Island. They starved between the Matty Islands and Agigigtuuq

– Greenland. I never heard much more. I never heard where they were going. I grew up just with a father and a father tells less stories. Maybe if I'd had a mother, I would have known more stories.'

One of Gibson's reasons for rejecting the story of a sunken vessel in the Matty Islands was that no skeletons had been found there. But our interpreter Louise Anaija said her brother had found a skull on Matty Island the year before, whether an Inuit skull or a white man's could not be ascertained.

Lena Kingmiatook, of Taloyoak, told her story as a continuation of the dramatic summoning of Pamiuluq, the spirit with the bad tail, to break up Parry's ship after Parry's flogging of the shaman during his sojourn in Igloolik. But in spite of Pamiuluq's bad tail, Parry's vessels and crews returned safely to home port. Lena's chronicle diverges dramatically here from the flogging story and becomes a tale of disaster. Lena associates her story with Haviktalik – 'the place having metal.'

'When they were getting ready to leave, the white men were all excited, they were heading back where they came from because they couldn't travel the way they wanted to go. While they were getting ready, even though the weather was so calm, pieces of wood started coming out from under the boat. Floating up. Pamiuluq, the one with the bad tail, was chewing up the boat, taking those pieces of wood out from under the water. The white people didn't notice their ship was breaking apart; the captain didn't notice either. They were excited, unusually excited, and they were cursed by the shaman not to notice. They were rushing, probably because they wanted to go while there was no ice in the area where they planned to go. After a while, when they were quite a way from shore, all of a sudden the ship broke apart. A lot of smoke, steam and smoke, came out of it. The weather was calm, so even though the ship was far away, you could see the smoke. We don't know if the ship had (auxilliary) engines but it probably did.

'A lot of these white people tried to swim to shore. Some of them sank into the water and drowned, and the water was so cold that some of them died of hypothermia. A few managed to swim to an island. And on that island they left quite a bit of stuff – a piece of wood from the ship and they also buried their important belongings.

'The Inuit met two survivors. We're not sure if there were other survivors but there probably were because they were able to bury their stuff. They had probably swum ashore, or if they didn't swim ashore because the water was too cold, they probably got into a lifeboat – on ships there are always lifeboats. They got onto an island and that's how the Inuit learned how the ship broke apart from those two white people.

'Those two white people who survived had seen Inuit living on seal, and they figured if Inuit could eat them, they would try to eat them too. When they took the skins off, the blubber was quite thick inside the skin and they used them to sleep in even though they were wet, not clean. They would put the skin on the ground and use it to wrap themselves up to keep warm. When they finally reached the Inuit, they were unrecognizable; they were so dirty. At first the Inuit thought they were demons or spirits, but when they realized they were not demons, they started helping them. They gave them new clothing and cleaned them up.

'When the white men had been in a big party, in a big group, the Inuit had been so afraid of them, but now there were only two left, the Inuit pitied them. They gave them new clothing, fed them and looked after them very well. Then the white men got back in their boat again and tried to go back to wherever they were coming from.

'And so the story ends and sadly we cannot tell any more. In those days, we didn't have a way of writing, but although we Inuit people didn't write stories, we memorized them and told them over and over so we could pass them down. Sadly the story ends here. We would like to know more about it, too.'

Late Evidence

Rather remarkably, there is support for the case that a ship sank somewhere to the east of King William Island in reports of an actual sighting of a ship in the ice to the north of Montreal Island, by members of the Anderson overland search expedition of 1855. These came to light only in the early twentieth century.

After John Rae's revelations, in 1855 the Admiralty made arrangements for the Hudson's Bay Company to send a small expedition, under Chief Trader James Anderson, down the Back River to verify Rae's findings and, if possible, search out Inuit witnesses. Incredibly, considering the effort involved, Anderson had no interpreter; however, he communicated with a few Inuit who had a few relics and who indicated by mime that these had come from a lifeboat and white men who had starved. On Montreal Island, at the mouth of the river, the expedition found several boat planks and a chip of wood marked *Erebus*. They were restricted by time and the need to return while travelling was good. They left in haste after somewhat less than ten days of investigation. They missed discovering Starvation Cove, not far away, where Inuit later told of many skeletons and a tin box which held papers. The journey supported, but added little to, Rae's discoveries.

Fifty years later, however, on 5 December 1908, the eminent Canadian geologist J.B. Tyrrell presented a paper to a learned audience called 'A Story of a Franklin Search Expedition,' later published in *Transactions of the Canadian Institute*.[17] He told a surprising story. In the autumn of 1890, while he was travelling up the east shore of Lake Winnipeg, a 'little old' man called Joseph Boucher, who had been cook on the Anderson expedition, came to his camp. He told Tyrrell that a ship had been sighted by a man of the expedition who was part of a small group sent out on an independent search, but that the man had returned and said nothing because he feared they would be required to go to the ship and, not getting home that year, all would perish of starvation and exposure. Anderson's journal for 8 August shows that a few men were dispatched with a Halkett boat. Boucher supplied the names of Thomas Mustagan, Edward Kipling, and Paulet Papanakies, the man who was said to have seen the ship. Mustagan was well known to Tyrrell. 'He was the chief of the band of Ojibway Indians which had its headquarters at Norway House, near the north end of Lake Winnipeg, and though rather old at the time was a splendid type of physical manhood, besides having a good reputation as an honest, industrious man.' Tyrrell did not know the others, but he found their whereabouts and in 1893 with the help of friends obtained three statements; Mustagan's and Papanakies' stories are of particular interest.[18]

Thomas Mustagan's Story, as Reported by J.A. Campbell: 'Paulet, Edward Kipling and I were sent off from the camp on the mainland in an inflated waterproof canoe to examine a chain of islands running far out to sea. There was open water between these islands and we proceeded from island to island, searching for remains as we went along. We found something on one of these islands, but I do not remember what it was. When we came to the last island but one, it was thought advisable that I, being the heaviest man in the party, should get out of the canoe, which was hardly up to our weight, and allow the other two to go on to the last island, which lay a long distance off. I was accordingly left behind. When my companions returned from this island, which was high and rocky, they reported that they had seen nothing. The expedition turned back shortly afterwards.

'After we were disbanded Paulet told me and others at Norway House that he had seen a ship from the lofty island in question, and that he had begged Kipling to say nothing about it, because, if it were known that the ship was there, an attempt would be made to reach it, their frail craft would be crushed to pieces in the moving ice, and they would surely perish.'

The interviewer notes, 'Tom goes on to say – "I believe Paulet saw the ship."'

Paulet Papanakies' Story, as Reported by J.B. Johnston: 'After saying the party left Norway House he thinks it was in the month of February, and other unimportant details, he goes on to say that a "Husky" [Inuk] who was fishing at the mouth of a river, the name of which he does not know, told him (Paulet) and Thomas Mustagan that a ship had been "ruined" and plenty people dead. They did not understand his language, but he made signs which they could readily follow and pointed to the place where the ship was all "broken." Paulet and Mustagan then proceeded to see if they could find anything, one going one way and one another, and it was Paulet only who from the summit of a rocky island saw quite distinctly what he still believes to be two masts of a ship. He says had there been more sticks standing around it would have been easy to have made a mistake, but there was nothing but rocks and ice as far as he could see. And in default of any kind of wood they were obliged to use moss on the rocks to boil their kettle. Upon my enquiring why he did not tell the chief of the expedition what he had seen, he replied in the most simple manner possible, "Well, I was tired of the whole thing, and was thinking long to be home, and was afraid if I said anything about it, we should have to go back and see what it was, so I thought I would keep it to myself yet awhile anyhow." And it was some time after that he related to some of his comrades what he had seen. Pieces of iron and wood, portions of a boat, were found in the vicinity of where they were then encamped.

'This was told to me in a quiet deliberate manner, leaving no room whatever to doubt his veracity, or the sincerity of his belief. He is by no means an enthusiast. He views the whole thing as one of his many experiences. He is the remains of a strong man, of unimpaired faculties, and still after so many years wedded to the belief that he is not mistaken in what he saw. I must confess to being very much impressed by the man's statement, knowing as I do that where eyesight is concerned how very keen an Indian is, and how they will detect objects at a distance which you and I would overlook twenty times.'

In his lecture, Tyrrell noted that these statements were given thirty-eight years after the events to which they refer. But he stated, 'That Paulet Papanakies believed that he saw a ship there can be little doubt, so the tale cannot be set aside as simply unworthy of credence.'

If Paulet Papanakies saw a ship – and in the light of Inuit stories this seems believable – where did she come from?

Tyrrell thought the ship that Inuit say sank in Oot-loo-lik might have drifted through Simpson Strait to a point where she was in vision before drifting back again. If we think outside the box, is it possible she was navigated there by a crew? Is it possible that after she had been looted by Inuit, Franklin crew members who had camped away from the ship were able to repair her sufficiently to sail her within range of Ogle Point? 'Depending on the wind,' says Michael Angottitauruq, 'this would take half a day.' (Inuit said that after the Oot-loo-lik ship sank, her masts were visible above the water. But perhaps here there is need for caution and the possibility of blended oral history: Netsilik Inuit from the Boothia Peninsula were prominent among those who passed on the stories, and Father Papion has told us that for many years these Netsilik visited the submerged wreck of Ross's *Victory*, trying to wrest off a mast visible above the water. Woodman notes that, confounding confusion, these important wreckage sites – O'Reilly Island, Cape Colville, and the Simpson Peninsula and Wales Island area – were all referred to in Inuktitut by the same name – Shartoo – the flat one.')[19]

Tyrrell thought also that Paulet might have seen a boat that had been dragged to the area by the retreating crews; but Paulet, asked if he could be mistaken, told his interviewer, 'It was a very clear day and I have seen the ship at York too often to be deceived.' Burwash considered the vessel – probably the *Erebus*, he thought – drifted down the west coast of King William Island and through Simpson Strait, and eventually came to rest close to Matty Island. It seems also possible an attempt might have been made to navigate her northeast around King William Island, taking her into the waters of James Ross Strait. Despite the Matty Islands hazard, these waters could have been navigated by Franklin's vessels. 'They would need fifteen feet,' says T.A. Irvine who as a young naval officer made a Northwest Passage on Canada's Arctic patrol vessel *Labrador*. Adds Michael Angottitauruq, 'Icebreakers do it.'

There are no shortages of possible resting places for Franklin wrecks. A story told in recent years on King William Island has it that a pilot flying over Chantrey Inlet believed he saw a submerged wreck in the waters far up the inlet below Montreal Island. Tommy Anguttitauruq believes this is entirely possible. He says, 'The tides and currents could reposition a wreck even from the Matty Island area.'

And stories of a wreck in the area of the Matty Islands persist. If there was a shipwreck in the area, were there survivors who made their way down to Chantrey Inlet? Or survivors who died struggling up the Boothia Peninsula and Somerset Island, dragging their wooden boats behind them? Such shadowy figures sometimes appear in the stories told of the Ross expedition. But the *Victory* crew was rescued by whalers.

A Record Lost

There is one more sad story. Matthew Tiringaneak, originally from the Back River area, told this story to Tommy Anguttitauruq: 'Tiringaneak heard it from his grandfather and his grandfather heard it from his grandfather. This great-great-grandfather went hunting caribou east of Chantrey Inlet about 150 miles south of Gjoa Haven and he saw an inukshuk he hadn't seen before. He decided to go and investigate and in this cairn was a lot of white and brownish-coloured material wrapped in a leather pouch – that was paper for sure. There were a lot of strange markings. That's writing. They were brownish coloured papers, not dark brown but light brown.[20] He figured these papers were cursed by a spirit who had left them there, and he took them and destroyed every last one of them.'

Sometime after Tommy told me this story, I met Tiringaneak in Gjoa Haven, and he repeated the story and added some details.[21] 'The man thought if he doesn't tear the papers up, he'll catch sick and die; or if not he himself, all his family will die. So he ripped them all to pieces and let the wind blow them away. They were wrapped up in something shiny like plastic, but I don't think they had plastic then. He didn't want to get sick, he didn't want to die, so he didn't keep anything. And that inukshuk, he tore it right down to the ground, so we'll never find any traces.

'Today Inuit might not have thought so, but at that time everyone thought he did the right thing.'

What mysteries might have been solved by those brown-coloured papers.

6 A Northwest Passage on Foot – and Lost Opportunity

 'I remember stories that people from around here would go up there to get things from the ship-wreck, even food like biscuits that were lying around,' the elder Albert Palvik of the community of Holman on Victoria Island in the western Arctic told anthropologist Richard Condon. 'They found a lot of stuff up there that had drifted up on the shore, like wood planks.'[1] This salvage came from the *Investigator*, abandoned in spring of 1853 on the shore of the Bay of Mercy on Banks Island, and a 'land store,' as Inuit say today, for the grateful Copper Inuit for half a century.

During the Franklin searches, a Northwest Passage of sorts took place. Commander Robert McClure lost his ship, but with his crew made a transit on foot. In despondent England, the news was cause for rejoicing, but, ironically, without this feat we would almost certainly know more about the Franklin disaster – why it took the course it did and how it ended – than we do.

In 1850, as part of the searches, the Admiralty sent a two-vessel expedition into the Arctic from the Pacific, the *Enterprise*, with Captain Richard Collinson as expedition commander, and the *Investigator*, under Commander Robert McClure. This was also the year that John Murray, publishers on Albemarle Street, London, brought out by order of the Admiralty, the *Esquimaux and English Vocabulary*. It was the first of several printings *'for the Use of the Arctic Expeditions.'*[2] In a handy phonetic self-help section, the *Vocabulary* instructed searchers how to ask Inuit they met the all-important question: 'Have you seen any big ships lately?'

In 1852–3, Richard Collinson wintered with the *Enterprise* off Cambridge Bay in the western Arctic. Inuit visited his vessel and seemed to come with news. Inuit often paid the *Enterprise,* he wrote in his jourrnal, 'casual visits, in which neither party, as yet could understand the other.' But with one group a subordinate made special efforts to overcome the language barrier. 'Mr. Arbuthnot succeeded in inducing some of them to draw a chart of the coast to the eastward, which was several times repeated, agreeing very well with each other, but were totally unlike the coast afterwards travelled over by me. He also appeared to think they indicated a ship being there; but in my opinion it was a repetition of his question.'[3]

Captain Collinson would rue that conclusion. Probably the *Enterprise* had with her the *Esquimaux Vocabulary*: perhaps it helped with the questions, but apparently not with the answers. Much more useful would have been the expedition's excellent interpreter, the perfectly fluent Inuktitut-speaking Moravian missionary, Johann August Miertsching. But Miertsching was on the *Investigator*, the expedition's sister ship, and whether by accident or design – a matter of debate – the vessels of the expedition had lost touch with each other.

Collinson bought from his visitors a number of articles 'which could have come from a boat or a vessel,' and by paying well hoped to encourage them to bring him more. And the expedition discovered other relics: in July 1853 two pieces of painted door frames, bearing the broad arrow, the Queen's mark, were found in Dease Strait on the Finlayson Islands; but Collinson was back in England before it was concluded that these came from a Franklin wreck.

What had the Inuit wanted to say? We know that 150 years after the *Enterprise* wintered there, elders in modern-day Cambridge Bay still retain their oral history. Did Collinson miss hearing of a ship at Imnguyaaluk or at Oot-loo-lik?

The Voyage of the *Investigator*

How did Collinson come to be stationed in Cambridge Bay without the *Investigator*, his sister ship, and without an interpreter, when a particularly fine one had been assigned to his expedition?

From the time they left England, the *Investigator* proved a slow sailer, lagging behind the *Enterprise* on the long journey via the Strait of Magellan to the coast of North America. The ships became separated on the journey out and failed to meet at Hawaii (then the Sandwich

The *Investigator* locked in the ice of Mercy Bay, Banks Island. Lt S.G. Cresswell shows a sledging party departing for rescue vessels on 15 April 1853. The crews of the *Investigator* were the first to complete a Northwest Passage, albeit by foot.

Islands), the resupply port. McClure came into Hawaii shortly after Collinson left; and then, taking a different route and with skilful navigation, arrived 'at the ice' off Bering Strait before him. Here, off Cape Lisburne, McClure met Captain Henry Kellett, optimistically stationed with the HMS *Herald* to greet the *Terror* and the *Erebus* should they emerge after transit of the Northwest Passage. Kellett had not met with the *Enterprise*, and McClure decided she had gone ahead of him. Kellett did not think so, but McClure declined to wait and speeded ahead. 'Certainly a very strong step for the junior vessel of an expedition to take ... and a great stretch of the power he accidentally possessed at the moment,' felt Major-General T.B. Collinson, who edited his brother's papers after his death.[4] McClure sailed past Russian America and entered the Beaufort Sea a year before Collinson, who retreated to winter in Hong Kong.

That year, McClure discovered Prince of Wales Strait between Banks Island and Victoria Island and spent the winter there, sledging up the Strait in October to the northeastern point of Banks Island and seeing with his own eyes the ice-choked waters of Viscount Melville Sound. If he could take the *Investigator* through the Sound, he knew he would have accomplished the passage. The following year, he made the perilous journey north up Banks Island's west coast – 'No idea can be formed unless witnessed,' he wrote, 'of the stupendous masses of ice with which this terrible polar sea is entirely filled.'[5] He found refuge for the winter on Banks Island's north coast in a harbour he named Bay of Mercy. This was a point only sixty miles across the Sound from Melville Island where William Edward Parry wintered in 1819–20. In the spring, McClure sledged over and left a record of the *Investigator*'s position at the marker Parry set up on his famous farthest west voyage.

This saved his life and the lives of his crew. The ice did not release the *Investigator* that summer, and McClure had to spend a second winter at Mercy Bay, during which his men deteriorated pitiably. McClure drove his crew hard. Both the interpreter, Miertsching, and the ship's doctor, Alexander Armstrong, pointed this out in their accounts of the voyage; Fergus Fleming, a modern-day chronicler of British nineteenth-century exploration, termed McClure 'obviously a little mad.'[6]

Fortunately for McClure, the note he left at Parry's marker before he realized he would spend a second winter at Mercy Bay, was found by an officer from the Franklin search vessels *Intrepid* and *Resolute* (under command of the same Captain Kellett, who had met McClure in Bering Strait). The vessels, despatched by the Admiralty to the west through Lancaster Sound were on the lookout for Franklin's vessels but also now, since there had been no news of them, for the *Investigator* and the *Enterprise*. On 6 April 1853 a relief party reached the *Investigator*. By then her crew had little expectation of survival. Dragging the ill on stretchers (there were three deaths), parties managed eventually to cross the strait to the search ships and safety. In doing so, they had circled the globe and walked the final link in a Northwest Passage.

The *Investigator*'s men had to spend another year in the Arctic before obtaining passage home, but Lt Samuel Gurney Cresswell, whose artwork depicts many dreadful scenes from the *Investigator*'s journey, was sent ahead with the official report. Sir Edward Parry heard the news of a Northwest Passage on foot and commented, 'My old quarters at Melville Island have now become quite classic ground.' Older and failing, he went to the Town Hall of Lynn to the ceremony to welcome Cresswell home. 'You see before you today about the oldest, and about the youngest of arctic navigators ... I came 200 miles and would willingly have come 2000 to be present this day. How little I thought, when I stood on the western shore of Melville Island and discovered Banks' Land in the distance, that in the course of time, there would come another ship the other way to meet me.'[7]

But from the point of view of the Franklin searches, McClure's triumph was a trade-off.

Collinson at Cambridge Bay

A year after McClure, Collinson followed his consort into the waters of the Beaufort Sea. He too explored up the west coast of Banks Island but retreated to the waters south of Victoria Island, where he wintered twice, first at Walker Bay, where an old man called Pamiungittok who had visited the *Enterprise* as a boy told the twentieth-century explorer Vilhjalmur Stefansson that the men from the ship had been good people who paid well for water boots and threw away much valuable stuff, which the Inuit picked up.[8] Collinson then sailed east to spend the second winter off present-day Cambridge Bay. In reaching this point, he had to take his vessel through a narrow waterway filled with rocky impediment. It had been explored earlier by boat and canoe, but the *Enterprise* at 400 tons was the first ship to sail through – 'a very considerable feat of navigation,' writes Ann Savours in *The Search for the North West Passage.*[9] From his Cambridge Bay anchorage, Collinson led sledging journeys searching for traces of Franklin. A good camper, he developed a recipe for 'fire balls,' a mixture of 'junk,' oil, saltpetre, and rosin, which, with the temperature at minus 30 degrees, started fires on the trail, thawing and boiling eight pints of water in half an hour.[10]

A Mystery Still Unsolved?

At the time of the interviews with Cambridge Bay elders during which Frank Analok told us the story of the ship at Imnguyaaluk, his friend Moses Koihok also reported the existence in the hunting territory of Cambridge Bay Inuit of strange inukshuks, mysterious cairns, which he believes should be investigated.

We know with certainty that on foot and by ship's boats many of Franklin's crew set out to reach the Back River. But did some choose another option? Did some crew members take boats and try to reach fur trading posts in the Mackenzie River area? The possibility exists. At the time of the Franklin searches, this was considered a much more likely line of retreat than the Back River. During the years of the searches there were rumours of the presence of travelling white men on the North American mainland and in Russian Alaska. Personnel from the *Enterprise*, and from the navy vessels *Herald* and *Plover* stationed in the western Arctic waiting for Franklin, made investigations, but the sources of the rumours seem never to have been satisfactorily established.[11]

Moses Koihok found the curious cairns on a trapping trip. 'It had been earlier said that there were high inukshuks – tall and flat – in the Padlikyoak area of South Victoria Island, and I wanted to check them out. On my trapping travels with my friend Kagetak, or Fred, we discovered three inukshuks – tall and made from flat rocks – facing west. They might have been white men's points of direction. Among the three inukshuks we found one that was made to look like a dog. That dog, especially, was made of very thin rocks – like shale. These inukshuks were skinny, and the larger one may have been a grave, though I thought it was a cache. I wanted to investigate, but my companion preferred not to disturb the site because it might be a grave. These inukshuks, probably built by white men, were pointing westward – in the direction of Holman. Those white men walked westward from there.'

Both Collinson with the *Enterprise* and McClure with the *Investigator* wintered on south Victoria Island at different times, and their crews might have built inukshuks in the style Moses describes – unlike those Inuit would have built. Or conceivably they might have been built by mysterious people long ago. Moses thinks they might be the work of qallunaat who lost their ship. Not far away are the Finlayson Islands, where the two pieces of painted door frames bearing the Queen's broad arrow were found. Back in England, these were thought to have drifted there from a Franklin wreck.

Moses Koihok talked about the strange inukshuks to Bill Lyall, son-in-law of Frank Analok, and many times elected president of the Federation of Arctic Cooperatives, the largest employer of Inuit labour outside government and government agencies. 'Bill Lyall wanted to see them by flying over by helicopter – but that's an expensive venture.'

Second Thoughts

Hampered by not having the extra manpower the *Investigator* would have supplied, Collinson did not extend his search past the eastern shore of Victoria Island. And it was at Cambridge Bay that Inuit visited his ship but could not make themselves understood.

In his print, *Return from the Seal Hunt*, Holman artist Victor Ekootak depicts life as he knew it in camp days. In 1852–3, Inuit hunters visited Collinson, wintering with the *Enterprise* off present-day Cambridge Bay and tried to impart news. But none on board could understand them. Holman, Victoria Island, 1965.

He was halfway home after the longest of all the searches – five years – when off the coast of Africa he heard from a passing vessel that John Rae had found indications of the Franklin expedition's fate. He recognized immediately what the lack of an interpreter had cost him. 'No doubt had we possessed the means of understanding the natives in Cambridge Bay we should have got a clue from them which would have induced me to pass over to Boothia [in fact, King William Island, or would he have visited the Royal Geographical Islands?] and examine its western face ... in which case the trail would most probably have been fallen in with.' By concentrating his forces, he felt, 'we should have been able thoroughly to investigate this locality in the summer of '53.'[12]

Collinson had cause to be rueful: his long arduous voyage had accomplished little that was new. Without the *Investigator*, the possibilities of his expedition were unfulfilled. On their return, McClure and the men of the *Investigator* received ten thousand pounds reward as discoverers of the Northwest Passage – in fact, one of them – and for the transit they made on foot. McClure received a knighthood. Amid the gloom engendered by Rae's report of death, starvation, and cannibalism, the Admiralty and the British public were grateful for positive achievement. While McClure returned to prize money and honours, Collinson's return was an irritation; some of his officers had been mutinous and Collinson wanted courts-martial, but the Admiralty declined to act. Collinson never undertook another command.

At an inquiry, he stated loyally that to McClure and his men belonged the honour of having discovered a Northwest Passage; the course McClure followed – his decision to proceed independently – was consistent with the instructions he had given, but he had never contemplated that McClure would reach Bering Strait before him and had given no instructions for that contingency.[13]

Opportunities to gather information from the Inuit were missed also by the next expedition sent to the Arctic, the Hudson's Bay Company's expedition down the Back River under James Anderson to verify Rae's information. Anderson had no interpreter and communicated only by mime. Would an interpreter have learned stories about the ship Paulet Papanakies said he sighted, reported to the Canadian Institute by the geologist J.B. Tyrrell only in 1908? Nor, despite its startling discoveries, was much information gathered from the Inuit by the Leopold McClintock expedition. McClintock had Carl Petersen, familiar only with the Greenlandic dialect, as interpreter. The possibly much-maligned Adam Beck told Charles Francis Hall, 'Carl Petersen no speak Husky (Eskimaux) quick – not good Husky speak – small speak Husky!'[14]

So a question continues to haunt: if Collinson's ships had stayed together and he had had the services of his interpreter, would we know more about the end of Franklin and his men than we know today? Inuit testimony about the ship at Imnguyaaluk suggests that we would.

With the Collinson and McClure voyages, the British Navy's involvement in the search for a Northwest Passage came to an end. Lady Franklin's private expedition – McClintock's expedition with the *Fox* – would provide some closure to the Franklin tragedy, but it would be fifty years before there would be a Northwest Passage by sea. This time the challenger would be a Norwegian: Roald Amundsen.

7 Norwegian Victory: 'Amusi' and the Prize

 Within easy sight from the centre of present-day Gjoa Haven is a spit of land where during a two-year sojourn the man Inuit call 'Amusi' – pronounced Amuse-uh – erected a marker. The marker eventually succumbed to community vandals or possibly the rigours of time, but Tommy Anguttitauruq remembers that in his boyhood he and friends once passed by the site and built the marker back up again. 'We called out, "Amusi! Rise up!" But the next year it was down again.'

Conquering Hero

In 1905 the news reached the outside world – and Sir Leopold McClintock was still alive to hear it – that the Northwest Passage – or one of them – had at last been navigated. The prize of centuries went, not to the British, who had expended so much life and wealth, but to the Norwegian Roald Amundsen. Six years later, Amundsen followed this up by besting Robert Falcon Scott in a race for the South Pole. Scott attained the Pole but found Amundsen had reached it before him. Scott died tragically, with his companions, on the return journey.

In victory, Amundsen was not ungenerous, at the time or later. For the transit of the Northwest Passage, he acknowledged his debts to British explorers, but after his conquest of the South Pole, sensitivities developed and Amundsen thought he detected undeserved *froideur*. He later reflected on this rather frankly in his book *My Life as an Explorer*, terming his competition 'a race of very bad losers.' Amundsen attributed much of his South Pole success to dogs (Scott had used ponies and some motorized vehicles), and at the dinner tendered to him by the Royal Geographical Society in London to celebrate his victory, he felt he received a 'thinly veiled insult.' Society president Lord Curzon ended his congratulations with the words: 'I therefore propose three cheers for the dogs.'[1]

On King William Island there are no such lukewarm sentiments. In the run-up to the centennial years of the historic transit – there will be community celebrations, Norwegian visits – Gjoa Haven people tell stories of Amundsen with particular verve, and with introductions from Tommy and transportation on his skidoo, I am fortunate to meet some of the storytellers in their homes.

David Aglurraq, known as Siksik, says, 'The Amundsen people were generous and even though a lot of the Inuit people stole from them, they didn't get angry. They were not like the qallunaat – the traders – who came later. When the Inuit stole from those qallunaat, they would likely get very angry and want to be paid back right away. The Inuit were probably quite a nuisance, but Amundsen still helped. He would know who did it, but he still helped even the same people who were thieves. Even today there's no one like Amundsen – the kindness, the generosity.'

David Aglurraq heard from his mother, a child at the time, how people on King William Island learned of the explorer's arrival at Uqsugtuq – 'where there is plenty of blubber' – today, Gjoa Haven. 'There was a man named Taraajuk [Amundsen spelled his name Teraiu] from the Koko Lakes area who was the first to notice that these white men were here. He went for a walk and saw tracks. They were very narrow tracks – not the way kamik tracks are, you know. So he went back and told his friends he had seen strange tracks – footprints on the snow that were very narrow. Some said they might be tracks of white people. Two days later people told their relatives they were going to see to whom those strange footprints belonged. They found the ship anchored in the bay here and they traded their clothing for knives and saws.'

The Expedition

Amundsen's expedition was a stark contrast to the earlier British naval expeditions. His vessel was a tiny fishing smack, and its crew travelled light and as much as possible lived off the land. Amundsen was born into an established family of shipbuilders and seafarers, and he dreamed as a child of becoming an explorer and making the Northwest

Passage. He had little personal wealth, but after some seagoing experience, he managed to find sponsors and acquire the *Gjoa*, originally built for the herring fishery, which he strengthened and fitted with an engine. 'The *Gjoa* was 72 feet long, 11 feet wide and of shallow draught. Naturally we had only one mast,' he wrote in *My Life as an Explorer*. At age twenty-nine, after meticulous planning, he set out to achieve his goal: to navigate the Northwest Passage by sea – 'the great adventure for which my whole life had been a preparation.'[2] 'What has not been accomplished with large vessels and main force I will attempt with a small vessel and patience,' he said in his diary.[3] He had with him six companions: his second-in-command, Lt Godfred Hansen (in later life, Rear-Admiral of the Royal Danish Fleet), Anton Land, Helmer Hansen, Peter Ristvedt, Gustav Juel Wiik, and Adolph Henrik Lindstrom.

In preparation, Amundsen had bought all the British explorers' journals: 'By reading these books I had thoroughly informed myself in the literature of my specialty before I made my successful attempt. A glance at the North Polar map will show that there appeared to be numberless possible channels threading the maze of islands off the north coast of North America. Superficially, it would appear that the obvious route would be almost due-westerly from the north end of Boothia Felix, where the map gives the appearance of fairly open waters clear across. This indeed was the route which most previous explorers had attempted with uniform lack of success. The distinctive characteristic of my successful venture was that I turned south along the west coast of Boothia Felix to the southern most point of King William Island, and proceeded on my way westward, closely following the coast.' In McClintock's *Voyage of the Fox*, he found 'a prophecy that the true channel would be found by following a more southerly route than that taken by the previous explorers. It was largely due to this prophecy that I adopted that route.'[4]

Amundsen took the *Gjoa* down Rae Strait and after difficulties in the Matty Island area reached the south coast of King William Island. 'Here we came to the most beautiful little land locked bay that the heart of a sailor could desire.'[5] By anchoring the *Gjoa* here, he founded Gjoa Haven.

The waters in the strait between King William Island and the Canadian mainland had been clear, and Amundsen might have sailed ahead and conceivably made the Northwest Passage that year. But besides navigating the Passage, Amundsen was committed to a program of scientific work. He had had to raise money to finance his expedition, and

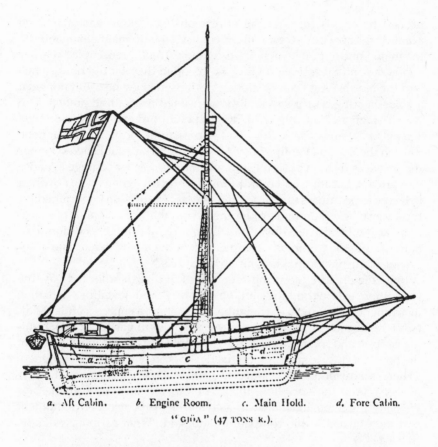

a. Aft Cabin.   *b.* Engine Room.   *c.* Main Hold.   *d.* Fore Cabin.

"GJÖA" (47 TONS R.).

DECK OF THE "GJÖA."

Amundsen's *Gjoa*. Built for the herring fishery, she was 72 feet long, 11 feet wide, and of shallow draught. Amundsen had her strengthened and fitted with an engine.

he had based his fund-raising efforts on his announcement that he planned to carry out investigations connected with magnetism and the magnetic north pole. Such investigations had preoccupied earlier explorers, and Sir John Franklin had intended they should occupy his. 'For the North-West Passage alone, Amundsen knew he could not get a serious hearing. For respectability he needed a scientific pretext. The North Magnetic Pole might do,' Roland Huntford explains in *Scott and Amundsen*.[6] James Clark Ross had successfully located the magnetic pole on the Boothia Peninsula, but it was still to be established whether the pole was fixed in position, and whether its area was a large expanse or mere dot. Locating and monitoring the north magnetic pole now had to be the expedition's first order of business. Amundsen had trained for this by getting a thorough grounding in the taking of magnetic observations at the Deutsche Seewarte in Hamburg; and the expedition 'had bought from the Germans a complete set of the most modern and accurate instruments for making our observations.'[7]

Immediately after securing themselves in their landlocked bay, the expedition set to building an observatory and installing sensitive instruments. They picked a height of land where a church stands today. Next was the job of provisioning: 'We went out in parties of two, hunting caribou and soon had piled up a hundred carcasses. One day, two of the boys and I were standing on the deck when one of them exclaimed: "There is a caribou!" He pointed to a small black object just on the skyline of one of the encircling hills. The other man, who had the best vision of the three, looked steadfastly at the black object for a moment and then turned to his companion and said: "That caribou walks on two legs."'[8]

The Inuit had arrived. In less than two decades, small craft not unlike the *Gjoa* would appear in Simpson Strait and white men, personified in the fur traders, would become familiar. But in 1903, on the part of both Inuit and qallunaat, there was a good deal of trepidation. 'Out in these wild regions where might is right, one never knows whether one is meeting friend or foe, so that it is best to be prepared,' wrote second-in-command Lt Hansen in a report included in *The North West Passage*.[9]

Amundsen watched as five figures advanced towards them. 'I sent the two boys for the rifles, and then the three of us advanced to meet them. I was in the lead and behind me came my little army of two. As the Eskimos neared us, we could see they were all armed with bows and arrows ...

'This began to look like a ticklish situation. We had no way of knowing whether their intentions were friendly or hostile. Certainly, they were equipped for war. The two parties proceeded to within about fifteen paces and then halted. I then turned to my "army" and instructed them ostentatiously to throw their weapons on the ground. I then turned to the Eskimos. Their leader, seeing this pacific move, imitated it by turning to his followers and uttering a command. They obeyed by throwing their bows and arrows on the ground. I was unarmed and advanced toward them. The Eskimo leader also came out alone.

'It is remarkable how accurately two men can communicate who do not speak a word of a common language.'[10]

The oral tradition closely follows Amundsen's account. Jimmy Qirqut, who told us the stories he learned from his father of Franklin's burial, also heard stories of this first meeting. His grandparents and his father, a baby, were camping at the time in the Koko Lakes area.

'The Inuit thought the tracks they had seen were probably tracks of white people. They found a place where these people had killed a caribou and skinned it and left the guts. The Inuit knew the bay here is a good place for a boat so some Inuit started off. When they were getting close, they saw the mast of a ship. A little closer and the mast and the ship were visible. Then two people started coming towards them. One was way ahead and the second way behind the front person. The first person carried nothing at all. He was walking towards the Inuit to meet them. He got closer and closer. Then the Inuit saw the second person behind, carrying a long stick. The first person started shouting to the person following him; he was probably saying the Inuit were not dangerous, not aggressive, not trying to kill him, but of course the Inuit did not understand. The person carrying the long stick put it down on the snow and also started walking towards the Inuit people. It was only later on that the Inuit found out the long stick was a gun. If the Inuit had attacked, that man would probably have started shooting them. The Inuit people, at least in this area, did not know anything about guns. They were probably afraid of meeting the white people but they knew they had to – so that the white people would not attack them. The white people were not aggressive so the Inuit were not aggressive either.

'The Inuit started walking with those white people to the ship. We think there were three Inuit people. They went to the ship with them and they got little gifts from them. We are not sure what they were. They got little gifts from them and they went back to the Koko Lakes where their families were.'

According to Amundsen, the Inuit were invited aboard ship and slept overnight. When they left, Amundsen asked them to return with caribou skins to trade. They arrived a few days later, and on their way home, Amundsen went with them, coming eventually to their camp of six igloos near a large lake. David Aglurraq's mother was a child in the camp. 'Amusi came to their camp to visit them. My mother had never seen a person with such a big nose. He did have a big nose, you can see by the statue in the community centre. They probably walked there and slept over.' Actually, Amundsen went on skis.

In Residence

'Taraajuk, who had been first to see the strange tracks, spent a winter with the qallunaat,' David Aglurraq relates. (The tracks belonged to Lt Hansen and another crew member, who had been caribou hunting around the Koko Lakes.) 'They arrived on Christmas Day and built their igloo near the ship.' Lots of Gjoa Haven people tell about what happened to this family when they ran out of seal oil for their kudluk. 'Amusi gave them some kind of oil – probably coal oil; something that burns pretty easily. The family used it for their kudluk and everything they owned became completely covered with soot. Their faces were completely black from soot – the only white part was the white above their eyes. When they walked on the snow, even their footprints were black!'

It was Taraajuk –Teraiu – who taught the *Gjoa* crew the art of igloo-building. Every morning after breakfast, they went over to Taraajuk's igloo and practised, using Inuit tools. 'We built in two parties, two to each. In 3 hours we had erected 2 magnificent igloos. We lack practice, which we will get later.'[11]

With Taraajuk encamped by the ship, other families began to arrive for four- or five- day visits. Sometimes, not far from the ship, as many as fifty igloos might be built, housing, Amundsen notes, 'about two hundred men, women, and children.'[12]

'Of course it was not very easy for us at first to make ourselves understood by these people. But once we had got them to see that our desire was to learn what different things were called in their language, the *entente cordiale* soon made rapid progress. Certainly we should scarcely have been able to keep up a regular ball room conversation with their ladies, but we acquired a vocabulary sufficient for our requirements. And we had no balls there.'[13]

David Aglurraq says Amundsen went easy on pilferers, but with a regular colony camped near his vessel, he took precautions. Amundsen knew to the Inuit the white men's metal – the knives, axes, guns – was beyond price.

'One question that the Lieutenant and I had discussed was how we could protect ourselves against the Eskimo, in case that they should take it into their heads to do anything. There was now a great number of them collected around us and if, for example, they were not very successful in their catches, our provision tent was exposed to them.

'We had, therefore, to teach them to regard us and ours with the greatest respect, and at last we hit upon a method of accomplishing this. A powerful mine was buried beneath a snow hut at a good distance from the ship, and a train laid from the ship and well covered with snow. When that was ready, we collected the Eskimo together on board. I spoke to them about the white man's power; that we could spread destruction around us, and even at a great distance accomplish the most extraordinary things. It was, consequently, for them to behave themselves properly. And not expose themselves to our terrible anger ... With a terrific report the igloo blew up, and clouds of snow burst high into the air. This was all that was required.'[14]

Not quite all. A little later Peter Ristvedt is again preparing 'a little mine at the door of the provision tent ... it would burst when the door was taken away. There was no danger from it but it would certainly have been enough to prevent any repetition of an attempt to break into the provision tent.'[15]

The little *Gjoa* was a house of wonders. Annie Aqvik is a wonderful Gjoa Haven raconteur, who sometimes tells her stories on the radio. She recalls the astonishment of her grandmother (her adopting mother) at the interior and fittings of the ship: 'When they were going inside, nobody touched the wall. It just opened by itself, and when they looked back the wall was solid, all made of wood. Then the wall opened again and they got into an area where there were already some visitors. Amusi's crew had a little toy. A wind-up toy. A little walking toy. You wound it up and it went walking around on the table. My mother knew it wasn't a spirit – you can't see a spirit – but it wasn't an animal either. Then my mother looked back behind her and a person was standing there. She smiled at that person and the person smiled back. That person was a woman in a parka and every time she looked at her the woman looked back. Every time she turned away, that woman turned too. My mother was looking in a mirror.'

The Inuit became regular visitors – according to reports, rather more than visitors. 'We had found Eskimo morality very excellent; even stern critics could not have found fault with their conjugal morals,' wrote Amundsen after he came back from a sledge journey. 'Now, on my return I found the most astonishing change.'[16] He says he took 'the first opportunity to have a most serious talk with my companions and urge them not to yield to ... temptation.'[17] But temptation was apparently great. According to Father van de Velde, OMI, the Oblate missionary who spent many years among the Inuit of the Arctic Ocean coast and knew the people who met Amundsen and his crew, 'Il parait que toute cette bande aimait bien les femmes eskimaudes.'[18]

Of this aspect of the *Gjoa*'s stay, David Aglurraq says,'There was a lot of sexual activity.' He adds, a bit crossly, 'That is when Inuit women became prostitutes.' Tommy is quick to help him. He speaks in rapid Inuktitut and then interprets: 'I'm telling him it's the oldest profession. It's not the first time it happened. The blades, the blades! All they had to trade with was themselves.'

In Gjoa Haven a number of persons lay claim to Norwegian heritage. Bob Konana says, 'I never heard it directly from my father himself, but when I was child close relatives would sometimes say, "Your father is a half white person – mixed with white."'

Konana, who can tell many stories of the old Inuit way, passed on an arresting account of an event still remembered with horror that occurred during Amundsen's visit. Amundsen provides the essentials in *The North West Passage*: 'Umiktuallo lived with his wife, three children, and a foster-son, in a tent pitched a few paces below the "Magnet." He had in his possession an old muzzle-loading rifle he had obtained by barter from another Eskimo. He had procured balls, powder, and caps from us. He was accustomed to leave the weapon loaded, which indeed in itself was not very dangerous, but in spite of our repeated advice he had not removed the caps. That evening, when he and his wife were visiting another family, his foster-son and his own eldest son got hold of the rifle. Then followed what so often happens when boys play with weapons without having been shown how to use them properly; they were ignorant of the danger, the gun went off, and Umiktuallo's son, who was only seven years old, fell down dead. The father heard the shot and rushed to the spot. At the sight of his own dead son, and the foster-son sitting with the smoking weapon, he was seized with frenzy. He carried the horror-stricken boy out of the tent, stabbed him three times, and then kicked him away ... Both boys were buried that night, we did not know where.'[19]

Konana's finely nuanced account of this tragedy illustrates Inuit attitudes of the time and suggests Amundsen and his crew knew they had to keep their guard up: 'When the crew heard the shots, they were right away on the shore with all their weapons. After they heard the shot, they were ready for battle. In those days if a relative was killed by someone, or even if a distant relative killed a closer relative, the Inuit would take revenge and kill the person who killed. That was the way to control mass murders; to keep the areas safe. If a person got angry and killed another, he would himself be killed.

'When Amundsen passed through here, it was still many years before the traders started coming up and people here could buy rifles directly from the store. The Inuit had only bows and arrows, spears and harpoons, and snow knives. The white man didn't come up here as early as he did to the east and western Arctic. So at the time Amusi was here the Inuit had no knowledge of rifles; so that is why the children were killed.

'When Amundsen was here, the Inuit had their igloos around the other side of the bay. He probably gave a rifle to one of those people. The qallunaat and the first group of Inuit they met trusted each other and helped each other so well. But later other groups came in and helped themselves to anything they could get their hands on – that was stealing. The first people never stole; they and the qallunaat helped each other and qallunaat paid them with whatever they had. Amundsen probably gave the rifle as a present. I'm not really sure whether it was given, or whether the people got it themselves, but a young person not knowing the rifle was dangerous, started playing with it, and accidently killed his playmate.

'Probably the Inuit were taught how to use the rifle, but they didn't know how dangerous it was. The father of the child who was shot said to the Inuit around him that he will not forgive the person who killed his child; he will not forgive or forget.

'He himself killed the killer; he killed the second child. Nobody stopped him. They were afraid of this man who had lost his son. So now there were two dead children.

'Amundsen and the crew heard the gunshots and probably knew something was wrong; but they were not sure; they did not know the children were dead. But when they saw the activity, heard the gunshots, they knew something was going wrong. The crew – there were quite a number – all came ashore with their rifles in the air.

'After the gunshot in the tent, they probably feared they would be attacked. But the Inuit didn't try to shoot them or attack them – there was no war. The qallunaat stayed on shore for some time and then went back to their boat.

'At that time there were not too many Inuit here; not too many capable of fighting. If the Inuit had shot directly at these white people, they themselves would probably have been wiped out – because there were so few of them. There was no animosity towards those white people, but that gun had killed the child.'

After this sobering story, Tommy says, 'I have seen the remains of one of those children. When I was waiting to be taken out to school at Chesterfield Inlet, I was staying with Father Henri. One day we took a walk and came across a skeleton. Father Henri told me the skeleton was the child the man had killed; the body had been buried out there.'

For some days after the incident, Amundsen said, they searched to find the graves of the children and eventually came across both. 'Each lay in his own grave surrounded by small stones on the hillside ... The son was carefully sewn up in deerskin and buried with his bow and arrows, drinking cup, gloves and so on, but the foster-son was treated very indifferently, his head was almost uncovered and only a pair of old worn-out gloves was buried with him.'

Jimmy Qirqut, whose grandparents passed the story on to his father, says he does not believe Amundsen ever gave a gun to anyone; but that a gun was given to someone by Atungela, a Qaernermiut Inuk 'who travelled through the area to visit the ship.' Atungela, the nephew of Chief Atungela, came from a family which had worked with the whalers, and his sojourn on King William Island is remembered well: Tommy Anguttitauruq recalls the story. 'When Atungela found out there were white people here, he wanted to smoke a pipe. He had traded with the whalers, so he knows what tobacco is. He travelled here some distance with people who had not met white people, and these people had no idea what tobacco was. It didn't make sense to people from the Netsilik area. They took three or four days walking to the ship. When they got close and saw the masts of the ship, Atungela started walking faster and faster and he got there before anyone else. When he came out, he was smoking a pipe, and the Inuit people wondered how smoke could come out of a person's mouth.'

Looking for Franklin Relics

During their sojourn on King William Island, members of the group made a number of local field expeditions, principally to further their magnetic pole studies, though they always looked for and sometimes found Franklin relics. Lt Hansen led four of these expeditions, the first in March 1904, to Richardson Point on the Canadian mainland, where Inuit had told earlier searchers they had seen remains.

On this trip, he was accompanied by Annie Aqvik's grandparents (her adopting parents), then a young couple visiting from the Netsilik Lake area of the Boothia Peninsula. Annie recalls their story: 'My father's name was Inukshuk and my mother was Qarlikla – later on, her qallunaat name was Nellie. They were on their way west to an area between Gjoa Haven and Cambridge Bay [probably the Royal Geographical Society Islands] where the seal hunting ground was a lot richer. That's where they were heading. But when they heard of the qallunaat, they decided to go and see what they could get from them, perhaps some qallunaat pots and pans.

'Amusi's ship was insulated with snow. You could see the wood but it was completely covered with snow. Inside it was very warm. The qallunaat gave them gifts – flour, rice, and some iron – knives and things like that. When they left with their flour and rice, they dumped them on the ground and took the bags. They didn't know what these things were. My mother always regretted that she wasted that good flour, but at that time she didn't know what flour was. Only later did she know flour.

'A few days later, my parents were told that Amusi was up here looking for Franklin or a shipwreck, and they needed some Inuit to go with them to Richardson Point or a little further on to look for the shipwreck. Amundsen's crew wanted to go with another Inuit family, but those people were scared of them and refused. That doesn't mean they didn't want to help them, but they were scared of them – scared to be killed by those qallunaat. My parents were probably also afraid, but they decided to help. They were young and they had no children, so they went along with two qallunaat over to the Richardson Point area looking for Franklin.'

Hansen noted in his account of his trip to Richardson Point in March 1904 that it was a demanding ten-day journey, and he and his companion, Peter Ristvedt, had to drag the sledge themselves, as their dogs were away on a sledge trip with Amundsen.[20] But in Annie's story there are dogs and dog food.

'They got on the dog team and took off with two qallunaat. When they camped, one of the men built two igloos. He made a hole through between the igloos, and my mother could see what the qallunaat were doing on their side and they could watch what was doing on hers. Then one of the men went out and came back with a piece of very shiny steel with a few things sticking out of it. Then he lit a match. He lit that piece of iron. She couldn't see a flame but it made a lot of noise. That was a pilot stove. My mother had never seen anything like that. She couldn't see the flame; it was making a lot of noise but it wasn't burning. Then the man got a very shiny pot and put snow in it, and it started melting very fast, faster than she had ever seen snow melt. It takes a long time to melt snow in the kudluk, but with the qallunaat it went fast.

'The qallunaat went to that area looking for Franklin, but they found nothing. They found nothing at all. Afterwards the qallunaat gave my mother and father presents. What they really needed were pieces of iron and steel, and they received a gift of a saw and also some ulus and knives and even needles and some food. Those white people tried to feed them, but they didn't eat those foods; they wouldn't put the qallunaat food in their mouths.

'After their journey with the white men, my parents travelled further west for seal hunting at the seal islands between here and Cambridge Bay. They did not return this way as at that time of year they had to travel fast before the snow melts and there is too much water on the sea ice. So when they were heading back to Netsilik, they probably travelled as fast as they could. They didn't stop by and never saw the qallunaat again.'

The Northwest Passage at Last

In March 1905, Godfred Hansen and Peter Ristvedt left Gjoa Haven on an eighty-four-day journey by dog team, surveying the coast along the sea route the expedition expected to take in its attempt to complete the Northwest Passage and exploring the last unexplored coastline of Victoria Land. Then on 12 August, after two years with the Inuit of King William Island, the *Gjoa* set out. Aboard was one extra crew member, a young Inuit boy called Manni, who had decided to accompany the expedition. (His relatives still live in communities along the Arctic Ocean coast.) The *Gjoa* now sailed the last unknown link in the Northwest Passage (no vessel had yet sailed through Simpson Strait – the waters of which 'do not deserve the title of "depths"'.)[21] 'He was observed,' says Frank Analok of Cambridge Bay. Amundsen reached Cape Colborne at the entrance to Cambridge Bay, where Collinson with the *Enterprise* had wintered. Collinson, wrote Amundsen, 'guided his great, heavy vessel into waters that hardly afforded sufficient room for the tiny *Gjoa*. But better still, he brought her safely home.'[22]

It was still not clear sailing, but now there were Collinson's charts. Then on 27 August, fifteen days after leaving Gjoa Haven, Amundsen, who was asleep in his bunk after being on watch, was woken by 'a tremendous running back and forth on deck. There was clearly something afoot, but I was merely annoyed they should make such a fuss for the sake of a bear or a seal. For something of the kind it must be. But then Lt Hansen burst into the cabin and shouted the unforgettable words, "*Vessel in sight, Sir!*"

'The North-West Passage had been accomplished – my dream from childhood.'[23]

The vessel was the *Charles Hanson*, a whaler out of San Francisco, and from her the *Gjoa* crew received the first news of the outside world. Since they left home, Norway had become an independent country. Soon they were in the western whaling waters, but they did not complete the passage that year. The *Gjoa* was stopped by the ice off King Point near the mouth of the Mackenzie.

While they wintered, the expedition lost two shipmates. Gustav Wiik, having survived all hazards of the Passage, died even though there was a doctor and rudimentary medical care at nearby Herschel Island. The expedition also lost Manni, the Inuit boy who was taken along for the journey. Gjoa Haven people still wonder what happened to him, but Amundsen relates his fate in his book. After checking on ice at a lookout, Amundsen and a crew member were approaching the *Gjoa* by boat when they noticed their flag was at half mast. They knew this meant bad news.

'The Lieutenant told me that while he was standing on deck talking to one of the lads, he saw Manni standing upright in his little boat, taking aim at a bevy of ducks. They were so much accustomed to seeing him under similar conditions that they took no particular notice of him. But a moment after ... the lad and his gun were gone.'[24] Manni had accompanied the *Gjoa* on the essential last link in the Northwest Passage but sadly did not complete her journey.

From King Point, Amundsen made a five-month ski trip – back and forth a total of thousand miles – to reach Eagle City, Alaska, and from there on 5 December 1905 he sent a telegram to his mentor the explorer Fridtjof Nansen. Amundsen had wanted Nansen to be the first to hear of his success, but Amundsen had no money and sent his telegram collect – $755.28 or $5,200 in present-day terms.[25] No arrangements had been made and the cable was stopped; the news leaked to the press and made Amundsen famous around the world long before its delivery. This cost Amundsen newspaper contracts which would have paid him badly needed money for a first-hand account of his victory.

He waited for mail and returned to King Point. Then, on 10 July 1906, the *Gjoa* made her way to open water and on 30 August 1906 at 11 p.m., in bad weather, passed Cape Prince of Wales, the eastern entrance to Bering Strait – 'We could just manage a little glass of whisky on deck in a hurry.'[26] They headed for Cape Nome and here offshore the *Gjoa* became becalmed. 'As daylight faded,' wrote Amundsen, 'we saw the lights were being lit in town, and our position was a very tedious one.' But suddenly a craft appeared. The crew on the *Gjoa* heard whistling, shouting, and cheering. 'So we had been recognized.'

Describing the last moments of his great voyage of exploration and discovery, Amundsen wrote, 'I really cannot say how I got ashore but a jubilant roar of welcome issued from a thousand throats and through the darkness of the night a sound burst forth that thrilled me through and through, bringing tears to my eyes; it was the strain of our national air – "Ja vi elsker dette landet" – Yea, we cherish this our country.'[27]

Amundsen would go on to become the pre-eminent explorer of the twentieth century, yielding his mantle only long after his death, at the dawn of the space age and the era of the astronauts. The prize went to a Norwegian, but in his victory telegram Amundsen declared he had made the passage 'in the tracks of Collinson.' In their quest of centuries, the British explorers had mapped the Arctic.

Back on King William Island, people continued to visit the bay where the *Gjoa* had anchored, and eventually the community of Gjoa Haven grew up there. Did the Inuit miss Amundsen and his crew when they left? Jimmy Qirqut says, 'We were nomadic in those days so we were not dependent upon them.' But nomadic days had only a few more years to run.

8 Modern Times

 Bibian Neeveeovak, senior elder on the Arctic Ocean coast at the time of my visit, has great-great-grandchildren who use the internet, but when interpreter Louise Anaija and I go to see her, she tells us, 'Qailirivuq' – 'It comes again.' 'That means "History repeats itself,"' explains Louise. With the Discovery Channel – Nunavut's favourite – playing in the background ('Inuit are so fond of animals,' says Louise, as a Siberian tiger stares at us from the screen), Neeveeovak tells us that when she and Louise's great-great-grandmother were young married women, they participated in the *first* communications revolution.

Perhaps in the later 1920s or early '30s, they travelled by dog team to Gjoa Haven to learn the Inuktitut syllabic system of reading and writing. 'The time we learned syllabics white people on their boat had gone into Gjoa Haven. They went there in the summer and wintered there. They had brought Inuit with them and the Inuit men had wives. The white men lived on their boat and the Inuit had canvas on land. We went there because we had heard that there you could learn.'

Was there a teacher? 'No,' says Louise. 'They learned from a piece of paper – a text. Whatever people would say, they would write it down quickly for practice. It got pretty silly at times but it went fast.'

'Each sound has a sign,' explains Neeveeovak, and in a fine clear voice she chants the syllabic table the way they used to do it to make sure it stayed in the mind. Did knowing reading and writing make a difference? 'A great difference,' Neeveeovak replies. 'It helped with everything. It was new knowledge.'

Nowadays

Two decades after Amundsen, and a long lifetime after Franklin's last crews died, the Northwest Passage became a reality, after all.

Under sail or with diesel, small vessels ploughed into the historic waters, charted at such cost: Dolphin and Union Strait, Coronation Gulf, Dease Strait, Queen Maud Gulf, Simpson Strait, Rae Strait, James Ross Strait. Many carried lumber, and in pursuit of white fox fur, traders set up trading posts. Slowly at first, and then with greater tempo, isolation retreated from the remotest regions of the Canadian Arctic.

Nowadays icebreakers, tankers, submarines, and sports vessels all navigate sea lanes through the Arctic archipelago. In 2004 *Fine Tolerance*, with Australian skippers Liz Thompson and Phil Hogg aboard, wintered in Cambridge Bay while preparing to try for the Passage in 2005. 'Before the big thing was to get through the Northwest Passage. Now that's not such a big thing,' Liz Thompson told *Nunatsiaq News*.[1] Modern technology has permitted the traverse of all the routes that thwarted nineteenth-century explorers, and the rapid ice melt caused by global warming suggests traffic will increase. (The *Globe and Mail* for 11 January 2007 reported Russia has urged Ottawa to make Churchill, Manitoba, on Hudson Bay a year-round port: their icebreaker fleet could do it, the Russians say.) Amundsen's route has become a working waterway, linked by the great Mackenzie to the 'end of steel' at Hay River on Great Slave Lake. It's a thousand miles down the Mackenzie and a thousand miles more to Taloyoak, last town on what is now the western Arctic shipping route.

I do my last interviews in Cambridge Bay, jump-off point for flights to the new towns on the Arctic Ocean coast that so recently were trading posts. In a few days, I'll fly home – five changes, but I'll reach my destination in twelve hours.

In the Arctic Islands Lodge, I hear again the stories Frank Analok, Moses Koihok, and Mabel Angulalik pass on 'from the generations before us' of the exploring ship at Imnguyaaluk in the Royal Geographical Society Islands and the ship that Inuit say they sank, perhaps with the help of shamans.

As a child, Mabel heard that her own relatives had come upon what they thought were pieces of a ship's wreckage buried in sand, she believes, to the east of Hat Island. Hat Island lies in the southeastern corner of the Royal Geographical Society Islands.[2] She gives credence to the idea that the shamans could have helped sink a ship. 'In the old days the shamans were looked up to for help. Their spirits gave them the power to do their extraordinary acts – acts which the ordinary person could not have done. In this case they might have used their powers to help the Inuit sink the ship.'

But according to Frank Analok and Moses Koihok, if, in fact, the Inuit of the day took defensive action, it was because of the great fear the qallunaat inspired. Even in their own youth, both explain, the white man was an unknown quantity. 'The traders came when I was a boy,' Frank says, 'and they were kind of scary at first.' Moses says, 'At first people feared the police when they came to the Inuit camps. They didn't realize they were here to help us.'

Mabel Angulalik has known the shamans all her life. As a child, she saw the great western Arctic shaman Alikamik healing her stepfather. 'In the past, the shamans were always at work, dealing with the unknown – with sickness and illness. They were not persons to be afraid of ... In those days we didn't have doctors, but the shamans had powers the same as the medicines we have today.'

Today the shamans and the spirit helpers are mostly gone. Long after the missionaries came – as early as 1771 on the Labrador coast and as late as the 1950s in parts of the central Arctic – shamanism and Christianity coexisted. In Taloyoak, Bibian Neeveeovak told me, 'In the past we didn't have doctors or nurses or expert people like zoologists to say why the animals were scarce. Sometimes the sealers couldn't make catches, so some of the shamans would try to see what was holding them back. We still have people who practise – towards Gjoa Haven and Pelly Bay – but a lot of them are dying out.'

The day before I fly home to the South, Mabel Angulalik points out that there is a magician at work in Cambridge Bay at this very minute. The community is in the midst of its annual Spring Frolic. There are community feasts and other special attractions, including a magician from Montreal.

That evening, I go down to the community centre and catch a performance. I sit by Frank, who speaks English, and we watch as the magician performs his magic, often helped by happy children from the audience. In his final act, he demonstrates how a knife can go into his body and leave him unscathed, just like the shamans of old. When the show ends, Frank shows himself the master of the one-liner. 'Super simple,' he declares.

The Continuing Search

Offshore from Cambridge Bay just over 150 years ago, Richard Collinson wintered with the *Enterprise*. Franklin search expeditions still arrive here today, but now they come to solve the last great mystery of the Passage – where are Franklin's ships? Despite the numerous searches and the advantage of all the great leaps forward in technology, the wrecks of the *Erebus* and the *Terror* have still to be found. Every summer sees new Franklin searchers. 'They come from Canada, England, the United States, and even Denmark,' says Pat Lyall, who has been searching himself with his vessel in the Matty Island area.

On King William Island, Inuit used to say that if you found a white man's grave, you'd never find it a second time – because it had ghosts around it. But this might not be true today, people agree, because Inuit now use the global-positioning system. Today on King William Island there are contemporary Inuit who would like to solve the mysteries of the Franklin tragedy, too. Michael Angottitauruq has tracked the fireplace trail (and believes it may lead him to new finds), while in Louis Kamookak, a board member of the Inuit Heritage Trust, Gjoa Haven has its best known on-the-spot investigator. With associates from the South, he has founded a group called 'Kamookak on Franklin's Trail: Ice Legacy,' which aims to make searches based on leads contained in Inuit stories and traditional knowledge. He made headlines when the *New York Times* for 5 September 2000 reported he led RCMP sergeant Ken Burton, skipper of the *St Roch II*, its crew, and some personnel from Vancouver Maritime Museum to graves of Franklin crew members who had died on Keeuna Island in the Todd Islands, thirty miles south of Gjoa Haven.

Sergeant Burton called the unburied skull and six graves 'a chilling reminder of how harrowing the Arctic can be.' The *St Roch II* was on a millennium celebration voyage that was taking her over the route of the RCMP auxiliary steamer *St Roch I*, which in 1942 became the first vessel after Amundsen's to complete the Northwest Passage.

Gjoa Haven residents say they have always known of the graves – 'Oh, my wife told me about them years ago,' says Rick Dwyer – but the Todd Island graves are not the only traces of early explorers Louis Kamookak has come across. He knows of other grave sites and he believes there is a trail leading to Matty Island from the western King William Island coast. 'It's there if you really look, but I don't know who made it.' There are important finds, he believes, waiting to be made.

These include Franklin's grave. 'My biggest feeling is that Franklin was left to be found. He's waiting to be found.'

Louis Kamookak comes by his interest in the Franklin mystery honestly. He's the grandson of HBC Gjoa Haven post manager Chief Trader Paddy Gibson, who both conducted Franklin searches and wrote about them. But Louis's interest was sparked, he says, long before he realized his relationship to Gibson. (Gibson died in an air crash.) 'It's always interested me. Even as a little boy of seven, I was fascinated.' Until the age of eleven, he lived with his great-grandmother Joanne Humuuk, whose colour photograph showing the traditional tattoos of the region on her face is on the walls of several houses I visit. 'I've got one in my house, too,' says Louis. 'She used to tell me stories about how when she was young she and her father were travelling on foot on the island and they saw a white man's grave. She didn't know it was a grave site: they didn't bury their dead back then. It was the length of a human and covered with gravel, real fine gravel, and near it they found a bunch of stuff. Her Dad found some sort of knife, a butter knife, something like that.'

Did they connect the site with the Franklin story? 'Yes, and the story stayed in my head. I thought, one day I'm going to find that site which my great-grandmother saw when she was young.'

Louis Kamookak estimates he has been conducting searches for over twenty years, often accompanied by his wife and four children. ('We were the last young couple in Gjoa Haven to have an arranged marriage,' his wife, Josephine, says.) He sets out fuel depots in early spring and searches later in summer on land with an ATV or with his boat.

Louis is in touch with Franklin investigators around the world. How do people find him? 'I don't know. I guess people give them my name.' He meets most of the searchers – they seem to turn up eventually on King William Island – and is a hospitable host. (Searchers can be competitive. On the 150th anniversary of the date of abandonment of Franklin's ships, Louis was commissioned to put up a plaque on behalf of the Gjoa Haven community. 'We were there at the point when some figures appeared.' Louis thinks these qallunaat may not have been overly pleased to find others there before them. 'Someone asked, "By whose authority are you here?" I told them, "By the authority of the community of Gjoa Haven." Eventually we shared a bottle of wine.')

In his house, Louis has many of the classic texts of the Franklin searches as well as more recent publications. Some books come through a friend, a book dealer in Calgary. Many are sent by his visitors. 'The books started coming in when people knew I was interested in them.' Superbly bilingual, Louis reads them and studies them in relation to the stories he has heard and taped from the elders.

'One reason perhaps there have not been solutions earlier is that Inuit have a fear of the dead, a fear of the spirits,' he says. One of his services to his community in the past has been to clear up suicides, to arrange funerals. 'There was an article saying the Netsillingmuit cut off the white men's hands to get at the watches. I don't think this likely because even today the Inuit are kind of superstitious about Franklin, about searching for dead people. It's one of the last things they want.'

By now Louis knows of every skeleton and bone recovered in the Franklin search area;[3] he knows all the theories and has his own theories based on a depth of knowledge of the land and the people not easily available to most Franklin searchers. He knows the stories Inuit tell. He knows how and in what directions the currents and ice of the Arctic waters can vastly reposition a wreck; how the water levels and erosion alter the shoreline. 'There's a place that used to be an island; now it's a point.' In the summer of 2008 Louis began assisting Parks Canada in a government-sponsored three year search.

But the Passage keeps its secrets for the moment. 'Oh, there's something out there,' says Pat Lyall. They'll find something one day, people believe, and interpreter Louise Anaija says, 'We'll hear about it on the Discovery Channel.'

Appendix One: Rumours of Hudson

During an interview with the author conducted by telephone, P.A.C. Nichols, former manager of the Arctic division of the HBC, passed on a story relating he believes to Henry Hudson, which he heard in 1938 while manager of the HBC post at Ward Inlet. 'There was one Eskimo who was quite well known at the time: Tegoodlerak – his grandson was later in Cape Dorset ... He was quite an old man, and he and I were quite good friends. He was at the post [Ward Inlet] with his family and I was there alone. He told me a story about Hudson. He said many, many years ago, a long, long time ago, in the time of his forefathers, a boat, a small wooden boat, came ashore, and in the boat was an old man with a long white beard and he died. But there was a little boy in the boat. They had never seen a little white boy before and they took him to their camp and fed him. The story goes that they tethered him to one of their end houses so that he wouldn't run away. And there the story ends. I tried to ask, "Did you ever know what happened to the little boy – whether he lived or died" – but he [Tegoodlerak] didn't know.'

Nichols noted that in pictures in books Hudson is always depicted with a long white beard. He added, 'What struck me at the time was that there were not too many white people mixing with the Eskimo – so that this was a story that was not introduced. It must have been passed down because it was too early for the white people to have recited this to him. In earlier times, those south Baffin Island people did go back and forth across the straits.'

Appendix Two: Charles Francis Hall and the Lost Men

Inookie Adamie has told us the classic oral history of the sojourn of Frobisher and his men among the Inuit. There are others.

Almost three hundred years after Frobisher's voyages, the American writer and Arctic explorer Charles Francis Hall found himself waylaid from 1860 to 1862 on south Baffin Island. He had come north on a whaler intending to make his way to the west coast of Hudson Bay to search for the lost Franklin expedition, some of whose members he believed might still be alive, living with Inuit. Circumstances forced him to alter his program and spend two winters on Baffin Island. He passed his time studying Inuktitut, travelling with Inuit, and mapping their country. To his surprise, he began to hear stories of white men who had long ago built a ship on Kodlunarn Island. Initially these seemed to him too improbable, but shortly he wrote, 'I began in my reflections to connect the Eskimo report with the time when Martin Frobisher made his discoveries.'

Hall began conducting systematic interviews with older Inuit, carefully writing down in his notebooks the information they gave him. When he returned south, he wrote this up in his famous book *Life with the Esquimaux*. From the stories Inuit told, he had come to a startling conclusion, one which still provokes lively debate among contemporary scholars. He believed that Frobisher's five lost men had survived in Inuit hands.

Hall had the best possible interpreters on Baffin Island: Joe Ebierbing and his wife, Tookoolito, also known as Hannah. They had been to England on a whaler and had met Queen Victoria; and Hannah particularly spoke fluent English. They became both his interpreters and friends and were closely associated with him throughout his remarkable Arctic career. Joe's grandmother Ookijoky Ninoo, perhaps around one hundred years old, Hall thought when he met her, was one of his most important informants (Inookie Adamie says he and his uncle Lucassie are related to Joe and descendants of Ookijoky Ninoo).

After listening to Ookijoky Ninoo, and others, Hall came to believe that Frobisher's lost men survived, lived with the Inuit for some years, built a vessel in the ship's trench, and masted it at Naparuqsivik. An alternative version of this story has it that not just the five lost men but a large number of white men wintered on Kodlunarn Island (some forty men were thought to have been lost with their boats and pinnaces when Frobisher's third expedition was battered by a great storm while leaving Frobisher Bay), were kindly treated by the Inuit, built a ship and masted her at the famous cliff, and then sailed away early in spring only (perhaps) to return and finally succumb to ice.[1]

Today's tape recorder–equipped collectors of oral history have to marvel at the meticulousness of Hall's note-taking and the material he was able to gather. He provides a remarkable picture of the Inuit life he became part of, but are his conclusions correct? Did, against the odds, Frobisher's lost sailors from the first voyage survive in Inuit hands? Was it the five men, still improbably alive after Frobisher's last voyage, or possibly even many men shipwrecked on the final voyage, who built, rather than repaired, a ship and then masted her at Naparuqsivik?

One difficulty in interpreting oral history is that, over long periods of time, stories often become blended together; and pinpointing an incident in time is another. Susan Rowley, a researcher who has made a study of the oral history Hall collected, and his notes and diaries now in the Smithsonian Institution, points out in her article 'Frobisher Mikisanut: Inuit Accounts of the Frobisher Voyages'[2] that his diaries contain records of interviews with twenty-five people, and that it is possible to reconstruct many different stories from the information he received. (Hall himself recognized that accounts would differ. 'I do not expect all will agree in their statements,' he wrote on 2 October 1861.) Nevertheless, Hall was convinced that all the stories about qallunaat on Kodlunarn Island and how they wintered there and built a vessel ('I never heard "built,"' says Inookie) related to Frobisher and his lost men.

While a few researchers consider that possibly the five lost men from the first voyage did survive, as Hall believed, others feel the facts lend themselves to different interpretations. Have old stories become blended together?

Before the great fleets of Scottish and American whalers began to gather off the coasts of Baffin Island – the era of eastern Arctic whaling officially started in 1817 when British whalers appeared north of Baffin Island in Lancaster Sound – there were documented whaling voyages up the Baffin coast. (Hall quotes a 1754 reference to Danish ships familiar with the coast and the ice above Hudson Strait for over twenty-five years in *Life with the Esquimaux*).[3] The late Joe Curley, who died in 1983 in Arviat, grew up on a whaler in Hudson Bay, but generations of his ancestors worked with the whalers out of Pond Inlet. In an interview before his death, he recalled, 'The first whalers spoke German [or perhaps Dutch or Scandinavian languages]. They came by a different route than the later whalers. They used to go through the Northern Quebec Strait before they came up to the Northwest Territories. Around the area of Pond Inlet when there wasn't too much ice, these ships would come in by a different route [than that used by British whalers, who crossed Baffin Bay] ... I've heard, some of those people came even from Germany.'[4] It seems possible that between Frobisher's day and Hall's, white men other than lost men from the Frobisher expeditions wintered on Kodlunarn Island.

In 1991 Susan Rowley did a provocative interview with Simonie Alainga, a notable Iqaluit Inuk who passed on a story he heard from his grandmother Jane Oo about a shipwreck that occurred beside Kodlunarn Island at a point called Tuapakjjuaq, 'the place of great pebbles,' on the mainland of Napoleon Bay.[5] 'They unloaded the ship there and placed it in a sandy area to repair it at Qallunaat; that is probably the time the name Qallunaat was given by the Inuit.[5] Today there is a big metal piece from that time still there. Then some people from Qasigiaraarjuk – "harbour seals" – and Qarmaarjuk – "sod houses" – [both local camps] used to go there and spend time with them ... probably just helping them survive.' (CBC producer Lisa Ell Ipeelie, who interpreted for many of the interviews with Iqaluit elders who passed on stories relating to the Frobisher expeditions, says, 'On the maps it's Kodlunarn Island, but older Inuit say "Kradluunaaqjak" – "where people saw white men landing."' Lisa Ipeelie checked with a number of elders to verify this point.)

The ship was lost offshore but 'the pieces were on the surface, so they put them together and they were building [them] back together there on that island. So when they were finished with the boat, they then took it to this point to install the mast; then the place later became known as

Naparutsiturvik – "the place where the mast is installed."' When Susan Rowley asked what happened to these people after they set out in their ship, Simonie answered, 'I have not heard the definite story, but they used to be thought to have gone to Iceland, but that might not be true.'

Sadly, Simonie Alainga died not long after the interview in a walrus hunting accident. When, during my interviews with Inookie, I ask him about the 'big metal piece still there,' Inookie tells me it was left by whalers.

Notes

Introduction

Inuit sources interviewed for this chapter include Kanyuk Bruce, Coral Harbour, 1983; Lena Kingmiatook, Taloyoak, 1994; Rosie Iqallijuq, Igloolik, 1998; Alice Anuttitauruq, Gjoa Haven, 1999; and Cathy Towtongie, Iqaluit, 2002.

1 Both Charles Francis Hall on his travels (see J.E. Nourse, ed., *Narrative of the Second Arctic Expedition Made by Charles F. Hall* [Washington: Government Printing Office, 1870], pp. 405–7) and the Schwatka expedition heard eyewitness accounts of the condition of Franklin's hard-pressed crews at Washington Bay. William H. Gilder reported that the expedition had learned from Ahlangyah, a Netsilik woman about fifty-five years of age, that 'some of the white men were very thin, and their mouths were dry and hard and black. They had no fur clothing on' (W.H. Gilder, *Schwatka's Search* [New York: Scribner's Sons, 1881], p. 91).

Meliki – his name is a corruption of 'the American' – worked for Americans as a whaler most of his life (see *Dictionary of Canadian Biography,* volume 13). I interviewed Cathy Towtongie, president, at the time, of Nunavut Tunngavik Inc., the Inuit corporation that oversees the implementation of the 1999 Inuit land agreement with the government of Canada, in 2002, and her grandmother Kanyuk Bruce, in Coral Harbour, where many whalers settled at the end of the whaling days, in 1983. Kanyuk told me that her grandfather had gone with Americans on searches for the lost white men, travelling overland from the Hudson Bay coast, but whether with Charles Francis Hall in 1869 or the Schwatka expedition in 1879 she could not determine.

2 See Dorothy Harley Eber, *Images of Justice* (Montreal and Kingston: McGill-Queen's University Press, 1997).

3 Sir John Ross, *Narrative of a Second Voyage in Search of a North-West Passage and of a Residence in the Arctic Regions during the Years 1829, 1830, 1832, 1833 ... Including the Reports of Commander, Now Captain James Clark Ross and the Discovery of the Northern Magnetic Pole* (London: A.W. Webster, 156 Regent Street, 1835), p. 232.

4 Vilhjalmur Stefansson and Eloise McCaskill, eds, *The Three Voyages of Martin Frobisher* (London: The Argonaut Press, Empire House, 175 Piccadilly, 1938), vol. 1, p. 48.

5 Susan Rowley, a member of the Meta Incognita Project, inter-institutional group investigating the Frobisher Arctic expeditions.

6 For a thorough exploration of this theme, see Rene Fossett, *In Order to Live Untroubled* (Winnipeg: University of Manitoba Press, 2001).

7 See chapter 1; and L.A. Learmonth, 'Ross Meets the Netchiliks,' *The Beaver* (Sept. 1948).

Prologue: Opening Salvos

Information for this chapter was gathered through interviews conducted in Iqaluit from 1997 through 2002 with elders Inookie Adamie, Lucassie Nowdlak, and Udluriak Inneak, all of whom had lived in family camps established for generations on the shores of Frobisher Bay.

1 Christopher Hall in Richard Hakluyt, *The Principal Voyages Traffiques & Discoveries of the English Nation Made by Sea or Overland to the Remote & Farthest Distant Quarters of the Earth at Any Time within the Compasse of These 1000 Years* (London, 1578; London: J.M. Dent; New York: E.P. Dutton & Co., 1907), vol. 5, p. 131.

2 Expert interpretation in Iqaluit was also provided by Leetia Janes. In Montreal, Pia Pootoogook and Papak Panegyuk provided valuable assistance, helping with checks on certain tapes.

3 Christopher Hall in Hakluyt, *The Principal Voyages*, vol. 5, pp. 135–6.

4 Frobisher carried back as captives a man from his first voyage and a man, woman, and child from his second. All died and are buried in English graveyards.

5 George Best, *A True Discourse of the Late Voyages of Discoverie ...* (London, 1578), in Stefansson and McCaskill, eds, *The Three Voyages of Martin Frobisher*, vol. 1, p. 50.

6 Ibid., p. 51.

7 Information from Tommy Anguttitauruq, grandson of Alikamik.

8 Dionise Settle in Hakluyt, *The Principal Voyages*, vol. 5, p. 145.

9 George Best in ibid., p. 217.
10 Thomas H.B. Symons, 'The Significance of the Frobisher Expeditions of 1576–78,' Mercury Series, paper 10, in *Meta Incognita: A Discourse of Discovery: Martin Frobisher's Arctic Expeditions, 1576–1578*, ed. Thomas H.B. Symons (Ottawa: Canadian Museum of Civilization, with the authorization of the Meta Incognita Project Steering Committee, 1999).
11 George Best in Hakluyt, *The Principal Voyages*, vol. 5, p. 265.
12 R. Auger, M. Blackburn, and W.W. Fitzhugh, 'Martin Frobisher's Base Camp on Kodlunarn Island: A Two-Year Time Capsule in the History of Technology,' in *The Meta Incognita Project: Contributions to Field Studies*, ed. Stephen Alsford, Mercury Series (Ottawa: Canadian Museum of Civilization, 1993), p. 74.
13 George Best in Hakluyt, *The Principal Voyages*, vol. 5, p. 265.

1. Into the Arctic Archipelago: Edward Parry in Igloolik and the Shaman's Curse

This chapter draws chiefly on the author's interviews conducted in Igloolik in 1998 with Rosie Iqallijuq and interpreted by Leah Otak. These are augmented by interviews recorded both with Rosie Iqallijuq and other elders for the Inullariit Elders' Society and held at the Igloolik Research Centre. All quotations from the Inullariit Elders' Society archives are identified in the notes by the archive file numbers in parentheses. The author has also quoted liberally from the following publications: John Ross, *A Voyage of Discovery, Made under the Orders of the Admiralty, in His Majesty's Ships Isabella and Alexander, for the Purpose of Exploring Baffin's Bay, and Inquiring into the Probability of a North-West Passage* (London: John Murray, 1819); W.E. Parry, *Journal of a Voyage for the Discovery of a North-West Passage ... in the Years 1819–20* (London: John Murray, 1821); W.E. Parry, *Journal of a Second Voyage for the Discovery of a North-West Passage ... in the Years 1821–22–23* (London: John Murray, 1824); Rev. Edward Parry, *Memoirs of Rear-Admiral Sir W.E. Parry*, 2nd ed. (London: Longmans, Green, 1865); Alfred Tremblay, *Cruise of the Minnie Maud: Arctic Seas and Hudson Bay, 1910–11 and 1912–13*, ed. and trans. A.B. Reader (Quebec: Arctic Exchange, 1921).

1 Parry, *Journal of a Second Voyage*, p. 269.
2 Ibid., 15 and 17 April, p. 425.
3 Mark Ijjangiaq, Inullariit Elders' Scociety archives (253)
4 There is also an Igloolik tradition that after Parry's departure the coffin was dug up for use of its wood. Information kindly made available by John MacDonald, Igloolik.

5 In this chapter, the author has quoted on a number of occasions from interviews with Rosie Iqallijuq in the Inullariit Elders' Society archives held in the Igloolik Research Centre, notably file numbers 26, 204, and 395.

6 For a full examination of Barrow's role, see Fergus Fleming, *Barrow's Boys* (New York: Atlantic Monthly Press, 1998).

7 Parry, *Memoirs of Rear-Admiral Sir W.E. Parry*, p. 54.

8 Ross, *A Voyage of Discovery*, p. 3.

9 Fleming, *Barrow's Boys*, p. 36.

10 Ross, *A Voyage of Discovery*, p. 34.

11 Parry, *Memoirs of Rear-Admiral Sir W.E. Parry*, p. 82.

12 Ibid., p. 85.

13 Parry, *Journal of a Voyage for the Discovery of a North-West Passage ... in the Years 1819–20*, p. 296.

14 Letter to Lady Bealy from W.E. Parry, 21 October 1825 (original in the possession of James Farfan of Baffin Land Books, 1400 Descente 20, Ogden, Quebec, Canada J0B 3E3, a copy of which was kindly provided to the author).

15 Rosie Iqallijuq, Inullariit Elders' Society archives (445).

16 Parry, *Journal of a Second Voyage*, p. 230.

17 From personal interviews with the author; Pitseolak Ashoona, Cape Dorset, 1970; Louis Kamookak, Gjoa Haven, 1999.

18 Mark Ijjangiaq, Inullariit Elders' Society archives (203). Ulluriaq, whose name means 'star,' was herself a shaman. Mark Ijjangiaq told the story for Igloolik's oral history archives of how when her grandson, whom she brought up as her son, went walrus hunting and was carried out by the tide alone with his dogs on the moving ice, he watched as – in the late afternoon, while there was still some light – Ulluriaq went up on top of the porch of the igloo. 'Her hood was tied in the middle and her "aku" – back flap – was also tied by the mid-section ... She stood up and hollered a number of times. This is what she said:

> "I summon the power of the stars!
> Ho, Ho Ullirijaat
> Ilaattaa!!Quunasiutinginnik Aturpungai
> Jaru! Jaru! Jaru!"

'Then she made a motion with her right arm as if she was motioning someone to come forward. As it turns out, she was doing "Quunasiuqtuq" ... something to do with using the stars for some form of magic power, and of course she too was named for a star ... Late that night when it was already dark, we heard him coming with his dog team.'

Ijjangiaq remembered that the next winter, though Ulluriaq was a prac-
tising shaman, she agreed to be baptized by the Catholic missionary who
had begun to visit the camps. 'I guess she found the experience pretty powerful, combining the Christian faith to her shamanistic practices.' And after
the baptismal service in the snowhouse, as the congregation watched, Ijjangiaq says, she began to sing and do her shamanistic rituals. 'Her helping
spirits intervened.'

19 Graham W. Rowley, *Cold Comfort: My Love Affair with the Arctic* (Montreal
    and Kingston: McGill-Queen's University Press, 1996), p. 217.
20 Parry, *Journal of a Second Voyage*, p. 270.
21 Cognoscenti who have visited the site in recent times have claimed to be
    able to distinguish between the qallunaat camp and the Inuit. The area,
    however, has been subjected to considerable disturbance, since Inuit on
    occasion have gone there on treasure hunts, bringing shovels to see if they
    could find any belongings left behind by the white men.
22 Parry, *Journal of a Second Voyage*, pp. 439–40.
23 Dorothy Harley Eber, 'Eva Talooki: Her Tribute to Seed Beads, Long Time
    Jewels of the Arctic," *Inuit Art Quarterly* (Spring 2004); Parry, *Journal of a
    Second Voyage*, pp. 270–2.
24 From 'Tattooing, a Discussion of the Practice across Arctic Regions,' in *The
    Greenland Mummies*, ed. Jens Pederhart Hansen, Jorgen Meldgaard, and Jor-
    gen Nordqvist (Montreal and Kingston: McGill-Queen's University Press,
    1991; originally published by Christian Ejlers Forlag, Copenhagen, and by
    the Greenland Museum, Nuuk, 1985). Peter Pitseolak of Cape Dorset, who
    took photographs and chronicled his community's history in *People from
    Our Side*, told the author, 'I've always heard it [the practice] was done so
    the women wouldn't get lost after they were dead.'
25 Bernadette Driscoll, *The Inuit Amoutik: I Like My Hood to Be Full* (Winnipeg:
    Winnipeg Art Gallery, 1980); 'Sapangat: Inuit Beadwork in the Canadian
    Arctic,' in *Expedition: The University Museum Magazine of Archaeology/
    Anthropology* [University of Pennsylvania] (Winter 1984).
26 Parry was instructed to set up the flagstaff with buried information on the
    ship's whereabouts in case John Franklin, exploring the waters off the con-
    tinental mainland, should come that way (W. Mogg, manuscript journal,
    1821–3 [original journal at the Library of the University of Southampton,
    Southampton, England], quoted in John MacDonald, 'Parry's Flagstaff near
    Igloolik, Northwest Territories,' *Arctic* 48 [Sept. 1992]: 308–12).
27 Parry, *Journal of a Second Voyage*, pp. 410–12.
28 Nourse, ed., *Narrative of the Second Arctic Expedition Made by Charles F. Hall*,
    pp. 112–14.

29 Herve Paniaq, Inullariit Elders' Society archives (141).
30 Pauli Kunnuk, Inullariit Elders' Society archives (087).
31 Mark Ijjangiaq, Inullariit Elders' Society archives (86).
32 Noah Piugaattuk, Inullariit Elders' Society archives (011) (59) (64) (228) (248) (60).
33 Tremblay, *Cruise of the Minnie Maud*, p. 153.
34 Noah Piugaattuk, Inullariit Elders' Society archives (303).
35 Inuit in North Baffin came to consider the free trader Robert Janes a danger to their lives. Because of the First World War, his associates failed to arrive to pick him up and Inuit became increasingly fearful – 'He had gone insane because he had so much to think about,' an Igloolik Inuk noted. A decision was made to execute him, and Nuqallaq carried out the task. He was rewarded for the execution by fellow Inuit but was charged with murder under the Canadian justice system and served part of a jail sentence before being released and returned to the community, where he shortly died from TB, probably having become infected while in jail.
36 Captain Robert Abram Bartlett, with his famous vessel *Effie M. Morrissey*, visited western Baffin in 1927, but he sailed through Hudson Strait and across Foxe Basin to the Strait of Fury and Hecla only in 1933.
37 Hubert Amarualik, Inullariit Elders' Society archives (252).
38 Rosie Iqallijuq, Inullariit Elders' Society archives (395).

2. John Ross at Kablunaaqhiuvik – the 'Place for Meeting White People'

Among Inuit interviewed for this chapter are Bibian Neeveeovak (interpreter, Louise Anaija), Taloyoak, 1999; Lena Kingmiatook (interpreter, Tommy Anguttitauruq), Taloyoak, 1994; Jose Angutingunirk (interpreter, Christopher Amautinuar), Pelly Bay, 1999; Patterk Qagutaq (interpreter, Christopher Amautinuar), Pelly Bay, 1999; Otto Apsatauk (interpreter, Christopher Amautinuar), Pelly Bay, 1999; Gideon Qauqjuaq, Taloyoak, 1999; Rev. Ikey Nathaoraitok (interpreter, Elizabeth Nathaoraitok), Gjoa Haven, 2006; Simon Tookoome (interpreter, Nancy Tookoome), Baker Lake, 2000; Silas Kulluk (interpreter, Nancy Tookoome), Baker Lake, 2000. Others interviewed, sometimes on several occasions in person or by telephone, include Rick Dwyer, Gjoa Haven; Alex Buchan, Taloyoak; and Father Papion, OMI, currently of Winnipeg.

1 In hard economic times, girl babies were routinely sacrificed. Neeveeovak says the practice stopped only in the 1930s.
2 M.J. Ross, *Polar Pioneers: John Ross and James Clark Ross* (Montreal and Kingston: McGill-Queen's University Press, 1994), p. 68; see Jane Griffin (Lady

Franklin), Diary, 4 Feb. 1819, Collections of the Scott Polar Institute, Cambridge, England.

3 Ross, *Polar Pioneers*, p. 390.

4 John Ross, *A Voyage of Discovery ... for the Purpose of Exploring Baffin's Bay, and Inquiring into the Probability of a North-West Passage*, 2nd ed. (London: Longman, Hurst, Rees, Orme, and Brown, 1819), vol. 1, p. 4.

5 Ross, *Polar Pioneers*, p. 59.

6 An anonymous letter, of which Ross was the author, sent supposedly by Captains R.N. to *Blackwood's Magazine* for April 1827 (quoted in Ross, *Polar Pioneers*, p. 113).

7 *A Treatise on Navigation by Steam; Comprising a History of the Steam Engine, and an Essay towards a System of the Naval Tactics Peculiar to Steam Navigation, as Applicable Both to Commerce and Maritime Warfare* (London: Longmans, 1828).

8 The British Navy did not adapt to steam as quickly as did merchant shipping (the first steam passenger ship was built in Britain in 1812), but the technical problems for fighting vessels were enormous. Steam vessels at the time needed paddlewheels, paddle boxes, and various propellers, much of this above the water line. This made a fighting vessel vulnerable indeed, and, in addition, wrote M.J. Ross, 'the boiler and engine rooms occupied nearly half the ship, and remaining space had to accommodate coal, ammunition, and the full stores of a sailing ship, for only sail could give the ship the necessary range ... In order to sail, the paddles had to be detached and the fires drawn, no easy task in heavy weather' (*Polar Pioneers*, p. 118).

9 Ross, *Polar Pioneers*, p. 124.

10 Ross, *Narrative of a Second Voyage in Search of a North-West Passage*, p. 94.

11 Lena stopped her story to say that she once saw an illustration of this incident and it matched the story exactly. Many people I interview mention having seen such a picture, but it seems likely to be of recent date. Matthew Tiringaneak of Gjoa Haven says Inuit know the explorers were artists. 'The way I heard it, those people – the explorers – drew a picture of him, so that's why everyone talks about his picture.' John Ross made many watercolour sketches during his sojourn with the Inuit, but on a visit to the Scott Polar Institute, where his watercolours are kept, I did not find Abiluktuq among them. The picture on p. 43 was drawn for this book by the contemporary artist Germaine Arnaktauyok.

12 Ross's original watercolour of this first meeting shows the Inuit lined up in rows as they advance, in keeping with both Ross's narrative and present-day Inuit oral history. The coloured lithograph made from the sketch in his *Narrative of a Second Voyage in Search of a North-West Passage* seems to show them in a circle.

13 Ross, *Narrative of a Second Voyage in Search of a North-West Passage*, p. 253.

14 Ibid., p. 256.

15 Ibid., pp. 264–72.

16 Ibid., pp. 272–4.

17 Ibid., pp. 272–84.

18 This story was told to Father Papion, OMI, and kindly passed on to the author. Personal communication, 25 March 1998.

19 Ross, *Narrative of a Second Voyage in Search of a North-West Passage*, p. 288.

20 Ibid., p. 591.

21 Ibid., p. 608.

22 Ibid., p. 643.

23 Ibid., pp. 643–4.

24 Peter Nichols kindly provided this information to the author by phone. Personal communication, 25 March 1998.

25 Ross, *Narrative of a Second Voyage in Search of a North-West Pasage*, p. 591.

26 Ibid., pp. 720–2.

27 Telephone interview with Rick Dwyer, Gjoa Haven.

28 Captain George Back, R.N., *Narrative of the Arctic Land Expedition to the Mouth of the Great Fish River and along the Shores of the Arctic Ocean in the Years 1833, 1834 and 1835* (1836; rpt., Edmonton: Hurtig, 1970), pp. 481–3.

29 Richard King, *The Franklin Expedition from First to Last* (London: J. Churchill, 1855), pp. 160–2.

30 Knud Rasmussen, *The Netsilik Eskimos: Social Life and Spiritual Culture* (1931; rpt., New York: AMS Press, 1976), p. 467.

31 From the transcript of an interview with Jessie Oonark and her children by Marion Jackson for the Department of Indian and Northern Affairs, Ottawa, 1983.

32 Simon Tookoome with Sheldon Oberman published the autobiographical popular children's book illustrated with his own prints *The Shaman's Nephew: A Life in the Far North* (Toronto: Stoddart Kidds, 1999).

3. The Franklin Era: Burial of a Great White Shaman

 1 The details of Franklin's burial and the burial of logbooks which Jimmy Qirqut passes on resemble in certain respects the story that one Peter Bayne, a whaler on the *Ansel Gibbs* who worked for a time for Charles Francis Hall, said he learned from Inuit with whom he hunted. Bayne heard that Franklin and his papers had been buried in cemented vaults. (When I ask Jimmy about cemented vaults, he says he has never heard anything of these.) A flat-topped mound was given as the site of burial. After his death,

Bayne's story, together with a copy of a map originally drawn by Bayne but lost, was purchased from a third party by the Canadian Department of the Interior (see L.T. Burwash, *Canada's Western Arctic* [Ottawa: King's Printer, 1931]).

Investigators have tended to dismiss the Bayne story. It has generally been believed that there was no contact between Inuit and explorers before the abandonment of the vessels in 1848 (which Jimmy's comment 'We don't know much at all' might be taken to support). David Woodman, in *Unravelling the Franklin Mystery* (Montreal and Kingston: McGill-Queen's University Press, 1991), suggests the Bayne story relates, not to the death of Franklin, but to later funerals of officers that took place after the vessels were abandoned and then remanned. He writes: 'Bayne's account is remarkable in its detail and accuracy and contains too much internal consistency to be dismissed out of hand just because it poses problems for a traditional reconstruction of the Franklin disaster, a version which has no place for an Inuit visitation to the ships or a burial ashore' (p. 235).

An Inuit witness to Franklin's burial cannot of course be completely ruled out, and Inuit stories about the ship at Imnguyaaluk (see chapter 5) suggest there may have been fairly frequent contact with a Franklin vessel and her crew during which information could have been exchanged. A King William Island tradition of military burial and burial of records may have reached Inuit whalers on the coast and then, perhaps with blended detail, been brought back in the Bayne version by travellers to the region. Among others, these would have included the Schwatka expedition and its Inuit guides; and, as late as 1903 when Roald Amundsen was at Ghoa Haven, a Qaernermiut (sometimes called Kenepetu) visitor called Atungela, who passed through the area of Simon Qirqut's camp on his way to visit the ship (see chapter 7). The Qaernermiut were inland Inuit who during the whaling season went down each year to the coast to work with the whalers. In 1903 some were helpers for the Royal Canadian Mounted Police – at the time the North-West Mounted Police – as were members of Atungela's family, photographed during 1904–6 by pioneering photographer Geraldine Moodie (see Dorothy Harley Eber, 'A Feminine Focus on the Last Frontier,' *Arctic Circle*, Spring 1994).

While present-day searchers continue to look for graves and records, over time much physical evidence left by the Franklin expedition has become degraded or destroyed. By now, 'unfortunately, the effects of time and vulnerability have taken hold,' says Owen Beattie in his afterword to Heinrich Klutschak's *Overland to Starvation Cove: With the Inuit in Search of Franklin, 1878–1880*, trans. and ed. William Barr (Toronto: University of Tor-

onto Press, 1987), pp. 221–4. This also holds true for sites of the early
searchers, now difficult to determine as many cairns have been torn down
and examined, sometimes several times.

2 R. Cyriax, 'Recently Discovered Traces of the Franklin Expedition,'
   Geogaphical Journal, June 1951, pp. 211–14.

3 Ibid.

4 Royal Geographical Society Archives, King to Dr Hodgkins, 1836.

5 Franklin's instructions were that he was to enter Lancaster Sound, sail as
   far west as he could, and then in the vicinity of Cape Walker head south
   and to the west in the direction of Bering Strait 'as the position and extent
   of the ice or the existence of land at present unknown, may permit' (C.
   Lloyd, *Mr. Barrow of the Admiralty*, p. 188, quoted in Fleming, *Barrow's Boys*,
   p. 368). Should his way be blocked, he might venture north, in hope of an
   open polar sea at the North Pole – a feasible idea, it was believed, at the
   time. Franklin was known to have expressed the opinion that if he could
   reach the waters immediately off the North American continent (some of
   which he had surveyed himself), he would have accomplished his task.
   Nevertheless, the major thrust in the search for Franklin was north, much
   of it north of Lancaster Sound.

6 R.J. Cyriax, *Sir John Franklin's Last Arctic Expedition* (London: Methuen,
   1939), p. 75.

7 From the Franklin record eventually discovered in the cairn on the west
   coast of King William Island, it is known that the first summer Franklin
   navigated up Wellington Channel and circumnavigated Cornwallis Island,
   before wintering at Beechey Island.

8 Cited in Robert L. Richards, *Dr John Rae* (Whitby, North Yorkshire: Caed-
   mon of Whitby Publishers, 1985), pp. 105–6.

9 King, *Franklin Expedition from First to Last*, p. 67.

10 Ann Parry, *Parry of the Arctic* (London: Chatto & Windus, 1963), pp. 220–1.

11 Ross, *Polar Pioneers*, p. 375.

12 Quoted in Nourse, ed., *Narrative of the Second Arctic Expedition Made by
   Charles F. Hall*, pp. 334–5.

13 Cyriax, *Sir John Franklin's Last Arctic Expedition*, p. 156.

14 Ibid., pp. 75, 71.

4. The Death Marches: 'They were seen carrying human meat'

Interviewees for this chapter include Mark Tootiak, of Gjoa Haven, in 1999;
and Tommy Anguttitauruq, who provided the author with lengthy interviews
in Taloyoak in 1994 and in Gjoa Haven in 1999.

1 C.F. Hall also heard native reports that Franklin's men went down both sides of King William Island (Hall Collection, booklet marked 'May 8–11 the 1866' [box 8]; book 'B,' p. 146; cited in Woodman, *Unravelling the Franklin Mystery,* p. 86).

2 Cyriax, *Sir John Franklin's Last Arctic Expedition,* p. 167.

3 Nicholas Qayutinuaq to Tommy Anguttitauruq. Kindly provided to the author by Tommy Anguttitauruq, Gjoa Haven, 1999.

4 Nelson Takkiruq to Tommy Anguttitauruq. Kindly provided to the author by Tommy Anguttitauruq, Gjoa Haven, 1999.

5 Scott Cookman, *Ice Blink: The Tragic Fate of Sir John Franklin's Lost Polar Expedition* (New York: John Wiley & Sons, 2000), p. 174.

6 A tradition is thought to exist that in desperate circumstances, merchant seamen – and many north-country sailors had been recruited as crews and officers for the *Erebus* and *Terror* – as well as some officers (Cyriax, p. 38) had a practice of drawing lots if human sacrifice was necessary. Peter Pitseolak, Cape Dorset's historian, told of an incident (which might have owed something to qallunaat example) involving a group of starving Inuit before the turn of the century around Iqaluit in the south Baffin area, where people had had long contact with whalers: 'Sometimes starving people killed a person to eat. When they had to do this, they would pick a boss. He was not necessarily the smartest person but he'd be the boss of the killings ... It didn't matter who you were when the man in charge of the killings said, "I want that person." He had to be fat – to be a good candidate to be eaten' (Peter Pitseolak and Dorothy Harley Eber, *People from Our Side* [Montreal and Kingston: McGill-Queen's University Press, 1993], p. 21).

7 According to Tommy's story, it was deaths on Baffin Island that caused people to fear the white people, but people of the Back River may have known of other killings – the three men killed (unbeknownst to Back) on their river in 1834 by members of Back's expedition. These deaths, too, may have caused fear that the white man was 'dangerous – too dangerous.'

8 Michael Angottitauruq, Tommy's brother (note that the brothers spell their last names differently), has hunted in the area and seen the site. He says, 'The taboo is less important today but there's a fear that there may be a trigger in the rocks that on entry could cause boulders to fall.'

9 Cyriax, *Sir John Franklin's Last Arctic Expedition,* p. 180.

10 Noel Wright, *Quest for Franklin* (London: Heinemann, 1959), pp. 152–5; R.J. Cyriax, 'Adam Beck and the Franklin Search,' *Mariner's Mirror* 48 (1962): 38–9; cited in Woodman, *Unravelling the Franklin Mystery,* p. 57. For discussion of Adam Beck's story, see chapter 4, 'Omanek and Adam Beck,' in Woodman, *Unravelling the Franklin Mystery.*

11 C.F. Hall, *Life with the Esquimaux* (London: S. Low, Son, and Marston, 1864), vol. 1, pp. 66–9.

5. New Franklin Stories: The Ship at Imnguyaaluk

Sources interviewed for this chapter include Moses Koihok, Cambridge Bay, 1999, 2002; Frank Analok, Cambridge Bay, 1999, 2002; Matthew Tiringaneak, Gjoa Haven, 1999; Michael Angottitauruq, Gjoa Haven, 2005–6; Tommy Anguttitauruq, 1994- 2006; Pat Lyall, Taloyoak, 1999, 2005; Alex Buchan, Taloyoak, 2002–4; Rosie Iqallijuq, Igloolik, 1998; Bibian Neeveeovak, Taloyoak, 1999; Lena Kigmiatook, Taloyoak, 1994.

1 There are suggestions in the literature that the expedition crews routinely adopted the use of seal oil for cooking as Inuit describe. In his report to McClintock, Lt Hobson, who first found the all-important Franklin record in the cairn at Victory Point, noted examining the camp near the northern point of Cape Felix, which looked to have been used for some time before abandonment of the vessels, possibly for scientific work. It appeared to have been occupied by a party of about twelve officers and men. Near three small tents which lay on the ground were what Hobson described as three fireplaces. He also noted a copper cooking stove apparently made on board. See Cyriax, *Sir John Franklin's Last Arctic Expedition*, p. 132.
2 Sir Leopold McClintock, *Voyage of the Fox in Arctic Seas: A Narrative of the Fate of Sir John Franklin and His Companions* (Boston: Ticknor and Fields, 1860), p. 227.
3 L.A. Learmonth, 'A Divergent Opinion,' *The Beaver* (Spring 1969). Hall believed the name Oot-loo-lik related to the area around O'Reilly Island, but Chief Trader William Gibson, a longtime resident of Gjoa Haven, in his article 'Sir John Franklin's Last Voyage,' *The Beaver* (June 1937), said the name refers to Grant Point and the Adelaide Peninsula. This was Gilder's interpretation in *Schwatka's Search*.
4 Nourse, ed., *Narrative of the Second Arctic Expedition Made by Charles F. Hall*, p. 404.
5 Ibid., p. 593.
6 Gilder, *Schwatka's Search*, pp. 78–9.
7 Roald Amundsen, *The North West Passage* (New York: E.P. Dutton & Co., 1908), vol. 2, p. 61.
8 Rasmussen, *The Netsilik Eskimos*, p. 130.
9 Nourse, ed., *Narrative of the Second Arctic Expedition Made by Charles F. Hall*, p. 257.

10 From its internal construction, Bibian Neeveeovak and Louise Anaija of Taloyoak considered this song originally came from the Repulse Bay area and, because of the frequency of the *ayayaya ayayaya ayayaya*, was of late origin.

11 Major L.T. Burwash, *Canada's Western Arctic: Report on Investigations in 1925–26, 1928–29, and 1930* (Ottawa: Department of the Interior, 1931), pp. 34–5, 72–3.

12 William Gibson, Chief Trader, 'Sir John Franklin's Last Voyage,' *The Beaver* (June 1937).

13 Hall Collection, field notes, book 48; cited in Woodman, *Unravelling the Franklin Mystery*, p. 288.

14 Jack O'Brien, *Alone across the Top of the World* (Chicago: John C. Winston Co., 1935), p. 49.

15 Gibson, 'Sir John Franklin's Last Voyage.'

16 Prior to 1971, when the government mounted Operation Surname to encourage adoption of surnames to help with record-keeping, most Inuit had no last names.

17 Dr J.B. Tyrrell, 'A Story of a Franklin Search Expedition,' *Transactions of the Canadian Institute* 8 (1908–9): 393–402.

18 Interviews by J.A. Campbell and J.B. Johnston, in Tyrrell, 'A Story of a Franklin Search Expedition.'

19 Woodman, *Unravelling the Franklin Mystery*, p. 285.

20 Remnants of the expedition apparently tried to leave records along their route, but none have been found, though Inuit told of finding books and papers. McClintock came upon a cairn at Cape Herschel which he thought had probably contained a record, but this appeared to have been rifled. See Cyriax, *Sir John Franklin's Last Arctic Expedition*, p. 169.

21 Matthew Tiringaneak originally told this story to Tommy Anguttitauruq, who passed it on to the author in Taloyoak in 1994. See Dorothy Harley Eber, 'Rumours of Franklin,' *The Beaver* (June/July 1996). Tiringaneak repeated the story and elaborated on it in an interview with the author in Gjoa Haven in 1999.

6. A Northwest Passage on Foot – and Lost Opportunity

1 Richard G. Condon, with Julia Ogina and the Holman Elders, *The Northern Copper Inuit: A History* (Norman and London: University of Oklahoma Press, 1996), p. 30.

2 *Esquimaux and English Vocabulary: For the Use of the Arctic Expedition* (version #1; and version #3, in which *Arctic Expeditions* is substituted for *Arctic Expe-*

dition). Published by order of the Lords Commissioners of the Admiralty by John Murray, London, Albemarle Street, 1850.

3 Captain Richard Collinson, *Journal of HMS Enterprise on the Expedition in Search of Sir John Franklin's Ships by Bering Strait, 1850–55*, ed. Major-General T.B. Collinson (London: S. Low, Marston, Searle & Rivington Ltd, 1889), pp. 285–6.

4 Major-General T.B. Collinson, in Collinson, *Journal of HMS Enterprise*, pp. 347–59.

5 RGS Archives, cited in Ann Savours, *The Search for the North West Passage* (New York: St Martin's Press, 1999), p. 224.

6 Fleming, *Barrow's Boys*, p. 405.

7 Parry, *Memoirs of Rear-Admiral Sir W.E. Parry*, pp. 328–9.

8 Vilhjalmur Stefansson, *My Life with the Eskimos* (New York: Macmillan, 1913), p. 361.

9 Savours, *The Search for the North West Passage*, p. 231.

10 Collinson, *Journal of HMS Enterprise*, pp. 263–4.

11 Flora Hamilton Burns, 'HMS Herald in Search of Franklin,' *The Beaver* (Autumn 1963). Collinson also put a small party ashore in 1850 at a trading post in Russian Alaska to investigate rumours of white men in the interior (later assumed to be HBC traders). The *Enterprise* officer in charge of the party was killed in an Indian attack.

12 Collinson, *Journal of HMS Enterprise*, p. 399.

13 Ibid., p. 347.

14 Hall, *Life with the Esquimaux*, vol. 1, p. 66.

7. Norwegian Victory: 'Amusi' and the Prize

This chapter draws in depth on the author's personal interviews; Amundsen's two-volume *The North West Passage* (New York: E.P. Dutton & Co., 1908) and his *My Life as an Explorer* (Garden City, NY: Doubleday, Page & Co., 1927); and Roland Huntford's *Scott and Amundsen: The Race for the South Pole* (London: Hodder & Stoughton, 1979). Inuit interviewed in Gjoa Haven, between 1999 and 2006, for this chapter include Tommy Anguttitauruq, David Aglurraq, Jimmy Qirqut, Annie Aqvik, and Bob Konana.

1 Amundsen, *My Life as an Explorer*, pp. 71–2.

2 Ibid., pp. 37–8.

3 Cited in Huntford, *Scott and Amundsen*, p. 76.

4 Amundsen, *My Life as an Explorer*, pp. 60–1.

5 Ibid., p. 43.
6 Huntford, *Scott and Amundsen*, p. 71.
7 Amundsen, *My Life as an Explorer*, p. 44.
8 Ibid., pp. 45–6.
9 Amundsen, *The North West Passage*, vol. 2, pp. 326–7.
10 Amundsen, *My Life as an Explorer*, pp. 45–6.
11 Cited in Huntford, *Scott and Amundsen*, p. 97.
12 Amundsen, *My Life as an Explorer*, p. 47.
13 Amundsen, *The North West Passage*, vol. 1, p. 120.
14 Ibid., pp. 259–60.
15 Ibid., p. 287.
16 Ibid., p. 202.
17 Amundsen, *My Life as an Explorer*, p. 49.
18 Correspondence of Father van de Velde, Oblate Archives, Ottawa.
19 Amundsen, *The North West Passage*, vol. 1, pp. 212–21.
20 Ibid., vol. 2, pp. 291–6.
21 Amundsen, *My Life as an Explorer*, p. 51.
22 Amundsen, *The North West Passage*, vol. 2, p. 105.
23 Ibid., p. 125.
24 Ibid., pp. 266–8.
25 Huntford, *Scott and Amundsen*, p. 111.
26 Cited in ibid., p. 114.
27 Amundsen, *The North West Passage*, vol. 2, pp. 291–5.

8. Modern Times

1 *Nunatsiaq News*, 8 April 2005.
2 In *Canada's Western Arctic: Report on Investigations in 1925–26, 1928–29, and 1930* (Ottawa: King's Printer, 1931), Major L.T. Burwash gives an interesting description of the Royal Geographical Islands and of Hat Island: 'This group of islands, extending approximately twenty miles east and west, and fifty miles north and south, consists entirely of low, flat tables of limestone ... The islands themselves appear to have only shallow channels between them, no channel for a boat drawing more than six feet having yet been located ... They are low and flat except for Hat Island, so-called because of its silhouette.' Burwash notes that Hat Island has a good harbour at the easterly end, well protected by reefs, and he finds many signs of native occupation. Stone caches, evidently for caribou meat, were numerous, and the higher ground appeared to have been used as a burial ground.

3 Retired RCM officer Glenn Warner confirmed for the author that there are
some skeletons from Franklin's crews in the Cambridge Bay cemetery.
He believes they were gathered on King William Island and brought there
by early HBC traders. They lie in an unmarked grave.

Appendix 2: Charles Francis Hall and the Lost Men

1 Hall, *Life with the Esquimaux*, vol. 1, pp. 271–2, 299–306; vol. 2, pp. 171, 284.
2 Susan Rowley, 'Frobisher Mikisanut: Inuit Accounts of the Frobisher Voyages,' in *Archeology of the Frobisher Voyages*, ed. W. Fitzhugh and J. Olin
(Washington, DC: Smithsonian Institution Press, 1993).
3 Hall, *Life with the Esquimaux*, vol. 2, appendix 8, p. 347.
4 From an interview with Joe Curley of Arviat, conducted in Arviat,
Nunavut, by the author in 1983 and deposited in the sound archives of the
Canadian Museum of Civilization, Ottawa.
5 Excerpted from an interview with Simonie Alainga conducted in Iqaluit in
1991 by Susan Rowley and kindly made available to the author.

Illustration Credits

Ronald Amundsen, *The North West Passage*, 1908: The *Gjoa*

Anthropology Archives, American Museum of Natural History: Detail from Inuit map drawn by Teseuke

By permission of the Trustees of the British Museum: The battle at Bloody Point in 1577

Feheley Fine Arts Gallery: *Fishing for Arctic Char*, by Janet Kigusiuq

Inuit Art Quarterly: *Beginning a Journey,* by Hannah Kigusiuq, Baker Lake; *The Shaman Seeks an Answer,* by Mark Emerak, Holman; *The First Explorers*, stencil by Sowdjuk Nakashuk, printed by Jacoposie Tiglik, Pangnirtung; *Cold and Hungry,* by Stanley Elongnak Klengenberg, Holman; *Return from the Seal Hunt,* by Victor Ekootak, Holman

Library and Archives Canada: *Parry's Farthest*, C-132217; Lyon's tattooed woman, C-099264; North Hendon, C-038856; At the mouth of the Back River, C-097310; *Loss of the McLellan*, C-041309; *Investigator* locked in ice, C-041019

McCord Museum of Canadian History, Collections of the Notman Photographic Archives: 'Search for Franklin'

By permission of the Nunavut Department of Education: Two details from the map 'Nunavut: Our Land'

W.E. Parry, *Journal of a Second Voyage for the Discovery of a North-West Passage*, 1824: Parry's vessels at Igloolik

Prince of Wales Museum, Yellowknife: Gjoa Haven artist Judas Ullulaq, photograph by Tessa Macintosh

Private collection: *Beaded Amautik*, by Germaine Arnaktauyok, 2005; *Abiluktuq*, by Germaine Arnaktauyok, 2005 (detail also used on chapter openers); map by Christopher Weigel (1654–1725); oil slick illustration by Michael Angottitauruq.

John Ross, *A Voyage of Discovery ... for the Purpose of Exploring Baffin Bay, and Inquiring into the Probability of a North-West Passage,* **1819:** 'First communication with the natives of Prince Regents Bay, as drawn by John Sackheouse'

John Ross, *Narrative of a Second Voyage in Search of a North-West Passage,* **1835:** '*Victory* Stopped by Ice'; *Victory*'s crews rescued by the *Isabella*

Scott Polar Institute: Inuit portrait of Edward Parry

Maps on pages xxiii and xxiv created by Malcolm Cullen.

Index